HENHOUSE

guess what?

HENHOUSE:

THE INTERNTIONAL BOOK
FOR CHICKENS AND THEIR LOVERS.

CREATED BY

Buddy Wakefield
Stephen Snook

Published by Write Bloody Publishing
AUSTIN, TX / 2012

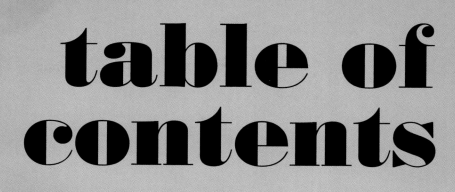

table of contents

PHOTO BY ASHLEY KNIGHT
(ASHLEYKNIGHTPHOTOGRAPHY.COM)

COVER PHOTO BY MYPETCHICKEN.COM

LETTER
FROM
THE
EDITOR

Why are we doing HENHOUSE? Because chickens run like little kids pretending to be airplanes. They stretch, completely. And sunbathe. They're funny and noble. We enjoy each other. There is care in all the eggs and the cleaning up and the room to wander. I appreciate what they teach us. Restful creatures. Reliable maniacs. We're doing this because our hens and Abner, the new rooster, would like art in their coop and stories for the neighbors and more ways for you to help hold up your end of the deal as a chicken keeper. We wanted to collaborate on a project with our chickens to create more awareness on healthy livin' for everybody. It was either build a book together, or start a band called Snowcapped Crap and go on a high school assembly tour, but the name is holding us back, so it has to be this: HENHOUSE. Welcome.

Some people call me the chicken whisperer because I take quiet dust baths and am spiritually connected to chickens. That's not true — it's sunny outside today and I would rather be having my me-maw's goiter embossed in wallpaper samples than writing "just another" chicken book, but something tells me you're gonna get more out of this than you expected. Besides, we have a thing for following through on projects around here. So we are, even with the distractions nipping at our heels (i.e. we recently got four ducks, two goslings and Abner). The hens have not yet expressed contempt, but I know they are capable of damage should anything try to intercept snack time. We are throwing more sunflower seeds to assuage them. We are staying on their good side so they won't get snotty during photo shoots. They are keeping an eye on all this new activity as it unfolds. So are we. We intend to let it unfold responsibly, to encourage folks who are jumping on the backyard chicken-raising bandwagon to know what they're getting into.

When I say "we," I'm referring to housemate/HENHOUSE co-founder, Stephen Snook, and myself. I'm Buddy. It's good to meet you. Steve's upstairs finding ways to carefully word an article about The Tyson Corporation so we don't get sued through a loophole for exposing heinous cruelties in their practices. I am downstairs listening to one of the red hens cluck, "Pick. Muh. Up. Pick. Muh. Up," over and over.

ALL LETTER-FROM-EDITOR PHOTOS BY INTI ST. CLAIR (INTISTCLAIR.COM)
ALL PHOTOSHOP WORK BY JASON BYRON NELSON (GUTTERPARK.COM)

Every time I try to oblige, she scampers off. I am certain she will reveal the meaning of life for us to include in this publication if I can just get close enough to hold her, and coo with her.

Here's what you need to know: no chickens were forced into any poses for the making of this book. Also of note, no one here is suggesting sex with chickens, despite the super hot chicken photos. Our publisher, Write Bloody, plants a tree for every single book purchased. HENHOUSE was inspired by hens with their wattles on the pulse, fowl photography and muther-clucking facts. While geared toward new "environmentally conscious" urban and suburban chicken keepers, HENHOUSE is made for everyone to laugh with and learn from.

Steve and I have only our personal experiences with chickens to guide us. We've had no formal training or education on how to care for chickens. We did have a lot of smart help, solid reminders and inspiring consultations from the fine organizations and chicken books that came before us, as well as outstanding text and photography submissions from good folks like you, who are also keen on respecting the lives of chickens. Special thanks goes out to all the not-for-profit chicken welfare groups for keeping their eyes on all things that would serve to improve or neglect the lives and considerations of chickens and other domestic fowl.

"I DREAM OF A BETTER WORLD WHERE CHICKENS CAN CROSS THE ROAD WITHOUT HAVING THEIR MOTIVES QUESTIONED."

Respect the chicken,
Buddy Wakefield

Dear Good Garden Hippies, New Urban Green Geeks and Redneck Vegetarians who may be considering life as a Chicken Keeper,

The backyard chicken-raising bandwagon appears to still be loading. Apparently, there's a lot of room. You may be as excited as I was to hop on in with great intentions. Rightfully so, if with healthy information, but I made some big mistakes when climbing aboard (like buying my first two chickens from a feed store, or pretending that properly caring for baby chicks would easily jive with my busy schedule). You don't have to be as naïve and unprepared. Below is a checklist of fundamental suggestions and considerations for first-time chicken keepers. Before committing to raising chickens or anything else in your backyard, do this:

THE FUNDAMENTALS

Make sure it's legal: If you live in an area that's unincorporated, contact the planning department to ask about zoning requirements regarding poultry. If you live in an area that's incorporated, contact the city clerk for information on ordinances regarding chickens. Note: there may be a processing fee if your local administrative offices have to pick up the phone, or use more than 23 basic words. Select city employees can be hypnotized with pleasant tones (not applicable to parking enforcement).

Be selective: Some breeds of chickens are sensitive to the cold. Chickens with large single combs are prone to frostbite. Make sure the housing you provide accommodates birds in both cold and hot temperatures, as per your climate.

PHOTOS BY JAMES DOBSON   (PEAKDISTRICTONLINE.CO.UK)

HEN'S HEALTH

PHOTO BY JAMES DOBSON   (PEAKDISTRICTONLINE.CO.UK)

Predator protection: At night keep chickens safe in an enclosure that prevents access by all predators, including dogs, raccoons, aerial predators, rats, cats, wild canines, weasels and Glenn Beck. During the day, house them in a fully fenced yard with proper protection from aerial, day-time predators, neighborhood dogs and — with regards to small bantam hens — large domestic cats.

Allow space: The predator-proof yard surrounding the coop should provide the chickens with secure access to sunlight, exercise, earth and vegetation at all times. The coop should include perches, clean and comfortable nesting boxes with straw bedding and posters of their choosing. Allow a minimum area in the yard of at least 10 feet by 17 feet per chicken, which equals 174 square feet per chicken. More space? Even better. Lack of space among chickens encourages feather pecking, cannibalism and disease. They do not thrive in crowded, stressful conditions.

Use care: A nearby veterinarian willing and able to treat chickens should be located before you acquire chickens. Veterinarians actually able to treat chickens can be very hard to find, depending on your community, but other resources include vets/scientists at local agricultural schools or universities, leaders of your local county poultry 4-H club, or known chicken farmers/experts/breeders at the local fair.

Respect the community: Have a prior understanding with your neighbors that you will keep X number of chickens confined to your own property and that the chickens will not disturb them. Let them know chickens never party at night, even on weekends.

PHOTO BY JACK WILSON, CHARLOTTESVILLE, VA

Legalize sanitizing: Use poultry dusting powder or liquid spray to control lice and mites on perches and other relevant areas. Some products are too toxic to put directly in the bedding or on the bird, so make sure you read instructions with care. Put diatomaceous earth in your flock's dust bathing area, and sprinkle it on the coop floor and nest boxes. Clean the coop and yard daily with a taping knife, rake and other appropriate cleaning tools. When a chicken house smells like excrement or ammonia, the problem is not the chickens. The problem is the chicken keeper. Filth promotes disease and suffering in birds, so keep it clean, like the following coop, which Ruby insisted on presenting.

PHOTO BY TERRY GOLSON (HENCAM.COM)

Provide vibrancy: Chickens love to stretch it out! Ensure they have daily access to sunlight and earthy material (e.g. dirt, peat moss) for dustbathing and sunbathing. Dustbathing and sunbathing are fundamental behaviors for the healthy maintenance of skin and feathers and the overall hygiene and wellbeing of chickens.

Discourage determined rodents: Grains attract mice and rats, big time. Feed should be kept in tightly lidded aluminum cans or other containers that make it nearly impossible for rodents, raccoons and other grain eaters to access.

Veto breeding: With the growing popularity of chicken keeping, the problem of unwanted chickens, especially roosters, puts a harsh burden on the birds as well as the animal shelters already over-extended with unwanted dogs and cats. Every effort should be made to adopt chickens from local animal shelters, relative online forums, or announcement boards.

Feed them well: Provide fresh clean food and water at all times. Offer plant-based seeds, grains, leafy greens, tomatoes and other vegetables. Poultry feed with animal byproducts should be avoided (it can harbor pathogens such as Salmonella). Vegetarian poultry feed can be purchased from feed stores. Consider buying local if possible. ChickenRunRescue. org suggests the following ratio for a chicken diet: 70 percent balanced pellet or crumble, 10 percent scratch and 20 percent fresh. This is a considerate, smart ratio. Some otherwise fantastic sites like C.R.R. recommend Purina products—don't do it. See KnowMore.org for more information on Nestle-owned Purina and the epic damage they've caused humans, animals and the global environment.

WHAT YOU NEED TO KNOW

Know your impact: As a result of the urban livestock/organic backyard-farming trend, shelters and sanctuaries in urban and suburban areas have seen increases (up to 780 percent)[1] in requests to rescue and place domestic fowl, particularly roosters. Hatcheries that are in the business of producing day-old chicks for shipment to residences and feed stores are backlogged with orders. When you buy birds from these hatcheries, most feed stores, or via anyone who uses the United States Postal Service to ship day-old chicks, you're unnecessarily supporting cruel behavior (see: Hens & Ammo, page 72).

Know your business: When animals are reduced to commodities, their interests are disregarded in favor of financial gain. Hatcheries producing chicks for backyard flocks treat chickens and their offspring in ways even we can't kid about. You can imagine the horrors. If you can't, the 13-minute film, "Glass Walls," narrated by Paul McCartney, is free and available to watch online.

Know the bigger picture: 50 percent of all chicks born in hatcheries are killed.[2] Urban and suburban areas generally ban roosters, yet male chickens comprise half of all chicks born.[3] Hatcheries use males as packing material, or "packing peanuts," in an attempt to keep females warm.[4] When individuals purchase chicks from these hatcheries and end up with roosters, they are then in the position of having to rehome or destroy the bird(s). Many are abandoned or dumped at shelters.

Adopt: Avoid perpetuating the willful negligence of hatcheries by adopting birds already in existence that need homes. Check out PetFinder.org for animals available at your local shelter. Visit Sanctuaries.org or FarmAnimalShelters.org and contact a sanctuary near you about adopting birds. Sanctuaries, shelters, online forums and bulletin boards at pet supply shops receive inquiries daily regarding animals needing homes. Ask that you be contacted if a chicken becomes available who needs a home, or post a WANTED bulletin of your own.

Stay healthy: Keeping the chicken environment healthy is important for the flock and the people. Stored feeds attract rodents who can spread disease quickly in an urban setting, so keep all grains and feed in metal containers with lids. Chicken droppings and molted feathers should be cleaned out of the coop and composted to help control mites and parasites in the coop. Properly composted feathers and dung make nitrogen-rich additive for garden plots and containers. Worming your flock twice a year is as simple as putting a worming additive in the water container. Diatomaceous earth is a huge irritant to mites and other skin and feather parasites. Provide this dusting powder for your chickens to dust bathe in, and use it beneath the straw or shavings to keep mites out of their nesting boxes and roosting areas. Fresh food, water and a clean coop go a long way in keeping chickens healthy; adopting these habits will sustain your bird's health and keep vet costs to a minimum.

Respect the chicken: Let the good intentions of urban chicken-keeping indeed prove good, not serve as an extension of factory farming. ∎

PHOTO BY BRAD WALTERS, SPRINGFIELD, MO

MARJA VAN VEENENDAAL *SPECTATOR* @FLICKR.COM

Jacques Pierre and
Gloria Glorifonzia

THE

URBANS

Name: **Jacques Pierre (J.P.)**
Hometown: **North Vancouver, British Columbia**
Breed: **Silver Duckwing bantam rooster**
Favorite song: **"Napolean," by Ani DiFranco**
Turn-offs: **Sissies.**
Personal factoids: **I'm pretty swo' for 6 ounces, so me and my lady friends hang with the "standard-sized" chickens in the free-range group where I live. I dream of driving a one-ton pick-up with a lift kit. Also, I hatched in a kitchen 3 years ago, thanks to Cale and Charlotte, my favorite kids in the world.**

Jacques Pierre with Henny Penny

PHOTOS BY JACLYN JULARBAL, NORTH VANCOUVER, B.C.

Name: **Gloria Glorifonzia**
Hometown: **North Vancouver, B.C.**
Breed: **Silver Chinese Silkie hen**
Favorite song: **"Wolf Like Me," by T.V. On The Radio**
A good book: **"Pole Dancing to Gospel Hymns," by Andrea Gibson**
Personal factoids: **I have dark blue flesh and bones. My rooster's name is Rusty. He's a graffiti artist. There are more bones in my neck (or any chicken's neck for that matter) than in a giraffe's.**

PHOTOS BY JACLYN JULARBAL, NORTH VANCOUVER, B.C.

Name: **Big John**
Hometown: **North Vancouver, B.C.**
Breed: **Black Australorp**
Favorite song: **"Your Protector," by Fleet Foxes**
A good quote: **"Will eat for food." – Mike McGee**
Personal factoids: **My kind came from Australia (you can probably tell by the accent). There's not a mean bone in my body, which is 25 inches tall.**

PHOTO BY: DENISE DAWSON

Jacques Pierre

PHOTO BY: DENISE DAWSON

Name: **Freckles**
Hometown: **North Vancouver, B.C.**
Breed: **Black Chinese Silkie hen**
Favorite song: **"Lay Lady Lay," by Magnet**
Turn-ons: **Soprano singers and banjos, dehydrated kale with cashew "cheese," Vipassana meditation.**
Personal factoids: **I'm exceptionally broody, which makes me a fantastic mother. If another mother abandons her young, I'm often happy to tend to them.**

Name: **Henny Penny**
Hometown: **North Vancouver, B.C.**
Breed: **Silver Duckwing hen**
Favorite song: **"Billie Holiday," by Warpaint**
Pastime: **Watching episodes of "Creature Comforts" on YouTube.**
Personal factoids: **I heard my keepers say of me, "She is gentle, quiet and likes sneaking off into the hay barn to lay eggs. Henny Penny will sometimes also lay her eggs in the Jersey cow's feed." I'm tickled by their kindness, but suspect they spy on me.**

PHOTOS BY JACLYN JULARBAL, NORTH VANCOUVER, B.C.

Bedtime with J.P., Henny Penny and the Girls.

PHOTOS BY JACLYN JULARBAL, NORTH VANCOUVER, B.C.

All thanks go to the photographers Jaclyn Jularbal and Denise Dawson, and to Courtenay Fraitzl and the chickens of Maplewood Farms (MaplewoodFarm.bc.ca).

BRO AD CAST ING

Three Reference Lists For New Chicken Keepers

TEN

Things You Will Likely Never Hear Your Chickens Say:

1) Hey, any chance we can sleep in today?

2) Oh my stars, I am so embarrassed about pooping on that. I'll get it cleaned up straight away.

3) So I just laid another egg. Really, it's no big deal, ladies.

4) I would like to offer you a fuss-free way of picking me up.

5) Oooooo, these new chicks are awfully cute. Let's throw them a housewarming — want to?

6) I have just had it with all these sunflower seeds.

7) No no, the place is so cozy, please, leave me in it all day. I can just watch my shows and drink diet soda.

8) Okay, I promise not to go near the garden again, in three minutes, again, after you just chased me out of there, again, with the water hose, again.

9) A personal bond? Oh, come off it, Chatters, what makes you think we wanna hang out in the sunny yard with you, or get excited to hear your voice, or feel the safety your presence offers? We prefer to be left all alone. Now take our offerings and be gone.

10) So you mean to tell me she just up and crossed the road? Well how had the egg already gotten there? Oh. Oh, that's a good one.

Proper Cleaning, Caregiving and Random Things New Chicken Keepers Should Cross the Street to Learn About, Buster, Because Other Chicken Books Don't Much Talk About Splatter-Proof Light Bulbs, Do They?

1) When you buy that heat lamp to keep them chickens warm, buy a 250-watt infrared bulb (constant white light can make trying to sleep a real challenge), and see that it's splatter-proof. There are several bulbs on the market designed to prevent shattering if contacted by liquids.

2) Keep a handy poop scoop for your coop. The metal end removed from an old hoe works nicely on the high surfaces. Just scrape it all off into a bucket and dump it in the compost bin. For the main floor of our walk-in coop, we use a taping knife securely screwed to a flat surface, then duct-taped to the end of a broom handle. It's lasted us a couple years, so far, and works perfect. Have a broom on hand too. Depending on the lay of the land, you might benefit from designating one pair of shoes for chore time.

3) We thought our 12-year-old Black Australorp hens were just growing kankles with age, but it turns out that — despite keeping a clean and tidy coop — those bumpy, lifted scales were being caused by scaly leg mites. The mite waste builds up under the scales. It can be pretty painful and eventually debilitating for your birds. You can treat for scaly leg mites by rubbing petroleum jelly thoroughly into their legs and under the scales. Treat it every three days for a few weeks. The scales may not return to normal.

4) If one of your birds fails to meet you at the coop for bedtime per the usual, don't panic. Listen. Have a look up in the trees or deep in the bushes. If she's young and in the tree, hopefully you're able to reach or coax her down. They get so cozy up there some early evenings that it feels wrong to disturb them, but if you want her safe for certain, keep her in the habit of roosting in the coop. Higher-ups in the pecking order may be encouraging her to "move it outside, sister." They'll adjust to one another. If she's deep in the bushes, she may be broody and building a clutch of eggs, having removed herself from the other hens in an effort to hatch chicks without incident.

5) The waste produced by one chicken in its lifetime can supposedly supply enough electricity to run a 100-watt light bulb for five hours, but so far we've only figured out how to compost it. Unless you're experienced with conversion technology, consider growing some beets and greens with your composted chicken poop. Chicken manure is a compost accelerator. Its high nitrogen content significantly speeds up the time it takes to break down your other compostables. If you're only composting the manure, add some old straw or woodchip

bedding so there's something to absorb all that heat to encourage the manure to break down.

6) "As a result of selective breeding and hormone treatment, the average broiler [hen] now takes 43 days to reach maturity, which is twice as fast as allowing nature to take its course. Ninety-eight percent of all chickens raised anywhere in the world — even organic ones — come from breeds developed by three American companies. More than half are Cobb 500s, developed in the Seventies by the Cobb Breeding Co. Seventy percent of Britain's broilers are processed by just four companies. The largest, Moy Park, based in Craigavon near Belfast, is part of the Brazilian food giant Marfrig, which supplies most of the meat used by McDonald's. Marfrig 'processes' an estimated 3.7 million chickens a day." —*The Second Book of General Ignorance* by John Lloyd and John Mitchinson

7) We know you know that chickens have ears, and that you can see their little earlobes hanging down below the feathers, but did you know the color of their ear lobes also clues you in on the color of the eggs they'll lay? Hens with white earlobes will most always lay white eggs (a rare exception is the Penedesenca from Spain, whose earlobes have white centers surrounded by red; they lay dark brown eggs). Hens with red earlobes can lay brown, blue or even green eggs. Silkies have dark-blue earlobes and lay pale brown eggs.

8) Chickens are omnivores. They'll eat seeds and insects, but also larger prey, like mice and lizards. We learned this thanks to the castoffs of our cat, Roger, who leaves a summer buffet of small land and air creatures lying around the property (if not in the living room). Sometimes a hen discovers one. She picks up the decomposing floppy thing with her beak, then she runs around like a celebration. Inevitably, the other hens go after her in hot pursuit of what's been discovered. It's a morbidly silly sight, like naked clowns dashing around the yard. Also of note: we learned that many cats aren't all that keen on tangling with rats, only mice and other small critters. Roger wants me to tell you he caught a bat once.

9) Chickens are smarter than my boss. They exist in stable social groups and can recognize each other's facial features. They adapt to newcomers. They have the ability to understand that an object, when taken away and hidden, continues to exist. More compelling is how they indicate something precise with each call they make (e.g. they have separate alarm calls depending on whether a predator is traveling by land or air). Even more compelling is their consistency and integrity. Next to Gregory Peck, a rooster may be the noblest example of a gentleman I've seen, and won't hesitate to put himself between the hens and a predator. Keeping chickens has made me wonder why being called a "chicken" ever had anything to do with cowardice. Chickens may have issues moving around permanent obstacles, or understanding what "stay off the porch" means, but they are otherwise sharp as talons.

10) "Down" is soft, fine fluffy feathers that form the first covering of a young bird, or an insulating layer below the contour feathers of an adult bird. If you buy feather pillows, or down comforters, jackets, clothes and other products stuffed with down, stay mindful of the fact that you are likely supporting the painful live plucking of chickens, geese and other fowl. Consider your hair being ripped from your head by the handful. Consider a flesh wound occurring from having your hair ripped out, then the offender sewing your opened flesh back up with no anesthetic. Consider being severely raw, and bleeding, then sent back into factory farm conditions after an afternoon of having your hair ripped out. Consider it happening up to seven times over the course of your short life. Consider watching this short YouTube video: "Goose Down Practices Called Animal Cruelty - CBS5."

11) Breathe deeply and listen close: make sure the coop you provide has more ventilation than you may think is necessary. Chickens produce an amazing amount of moisture, ammonia and heat, and are prone to respiratory problems. Ventilation (natural ventilation is the most foolproof) helps remove dampness and ammonia fumes, and keeps the coop from getting too hot in the summer. Securely screen the vents with hardware cloth or something similar so that predators can't tear it off, or climb between it, or grab handfuls of chicken through it. Remember that you're creating ventilation (even if you live in a cold climate), not direct drafts for the chickens.

12) Hens lay eggs when the days are long, then they slow production as the days grow short in winter. Why? Because daylight stimulates the pituitary gland, which stimulates the ovaries to produce eggs. Hens lay when they have daylight for at least 12-14 hours per day. Egg production drops off significantly and may even stop once the days become shorter.

13) They love small worms, insects and especially flies, but these things have a high risk of introducing internal parasites to the birds — yes, even worms have worms! It's not recommended to offer these treats into a chick's environment. Of course, in nature they will come across them anyway, so it's not the worst, but steer clear of strengthening negative chances.

14) Chickens pee, poop, have sex and lay eggs through the same orifice. That orifice is called the cloaca.

15) Chickens rarely complain when they're in pain, so they need you to proactively observe them and know their characteristics. I once picked up a chicken who was a bit off-kilter from the rest of the ladies. She had fresh poop and some blood matting down her backside. I'd picked her up to have a look. The smell was awful (a healthy chicken will not put off foul odor). What I saw was most disturbing; the blood and feces were not coming from her cloaca, but rather through a deep connecting wound that was infested with maggots. Be attentive. Supportive Inter-

net forums like BackyardChickens.com, and helpful folks like Terry Golson of HenCam.com, leave little room for excuses to not find the answers and support you require in understanding your chickens' health issues.

16) Chickens do not have teeth. They swallow their food whole. Part of their stomach, the gizzard, is used to grind up that food. A chicken's gizzard will likely have gravel to help break down the food for digestion. Several books will tell you that chickens know what's good for them and will not eat anything that will hurt them. While chickens are good at steering clear of foods with imminent health threats, they will tear through heavily processed food faster than HENHOUSE editors can devour a buttery pastry (heads up: that's real fast, y'all). Don't kid yourself; it is no more healthy for chickens to eat that junk than it is for you. Supplement their diet with whole grains and fresh produce. A healthier chicken is a happier chicken, indeed.

17) Chickens will be less reactionary toward your approach if — while tending to their pen or chicken house — you enter slowly with your back towards them. Our feathered crew loves to walk alongside us and hang out in close proximity, but they're not the biggest fans of being picked up or directly advanced upon. They sure appreciate any thoughtfulness toward their calm.

18) "In 2003, in the United States' Rockies, the 68-million-year-old fossilized femur bone of a Tyrannosaurus Rex was found to still contain flexible collagen. When the DNA of this protein was sequenced, its closest match was found to be that of the chicken, further bolstering the theory that birds evolved from dinosaurs, rather than other branches of the reptile family," *The Second Book of General Ignorance* by John Lloyd and John Mitchinson. On a relative note, all vertebrates have eggs, but the hard-shelled variety first appeared among reptiles. And, all domestic chickens can be genetically traced to Gallus Gallus, The Red Jungle Fowl (a member of the pheasant family native to Thailand).[5]

19) There are so many resources out there for furthering your education on chickens. Here's the basic lingo in case you find yourself seeking comprehensive advice on specific topics while in chat rooms or other publications: female chickens are pullets until they're old enough to lay eggs, then they become hens. Male chickens are called roosters, cocks or — if younger than a year — cockerels. A castrated male chicken is called a capon. Please consider not turning your rooster into a capon unless you plan on leading by example.

20) "If you're thinking of getting chickens also plan on getting [human] snacks. And beverages... The second you get chickens you get visitors. And lots of 'em. Most of them don't think to bring their own refreshments, and at least one of them will ask when the chickens will be ready to eat. Then they'll laugh hysterically at their own joke. Guaranteed." - Karen (TheArtOfDoingStuff.com)

FIVE
Films Your Chicken Hopes You Watch and Learn From:

1) Chicken Run (2000)
This one is definitely for the kid in all of us! A British stop-motion animation film made by the Aardman Animations studios, directed by Peter Lord and Nick Park. The film centers on a band of chickens who seeks a smooth-talking Rhode Island Red named Rocky as their only hope for escaping certain death when the owners of their farm decide to go from selling eggs to selling chicken pies. We chuckled out loud for the whole ride. If you're new to the world of chickens, take note: chickens don't really have teeth.

2) The Future of Food (2004)
Before compiling your next grocery list, you may wanna watch filmmaker Deborah Koons Garcia's eye-opening documentary, which sheds light on a shadowy relationship between agriculture, big business and government. By examining the effects of biotechnology on the nation's smallest farmers, this film reveals the unappetizing truth about genetically modified foods (the ones you likely serve for dinner).

3) Forks Over Knives (2011)
Focusing on the research of two food scientists, this earnest documentary reveals that despite broad advances in medical technology, the popularity of modern processed foods has led to epidemic rates of obesity, diabetes and other diseases. This is the film I find myself most recommending to folks with constant health issues and loads of convenient excuses for them.

4) Food, Inc. (2008)
Director Robert Kenner's provocative, Oscar-nominated documentary explores the food industry's detrimental effects on our health and environment. This is the startling film that most opened our household's eyes to the depth of our personal disregard for health, as well as the food industry's.

5) The Natural History of the Chicken (2001)
Chickens are as popular as ever and this endearing documentary sets out to uncover the truth about the bird that has touched the lives of so many. Included are amusing and often moving stories that may forever change your view of the chicken.

A CLUCKWORK ORANGE

CELEBRITY

Upon discovering at least three gorgeous hens bearing remarkable resemblances to Bee Arthur, and one sweet, sharp feller who reminded me of Patton Oswalt, we began collecting celebrity look-alike chickens. Here are some of our favorites:

LOOKALIKES

When Steve and I saw this stunning star hen impersonating Farrah Fawcett, we knew she had to be on the cover of HEN-HOUSE. Once, when I was a young boy, as a Mother's Day gift I wrote a note, put it in a paper bag, decorated the bag and stapled it shut for Mom to open. The note read, "You're as pretty as Farrah Fawcett." It was so true to me. Still is. Thank you, Farrah Fawcett.

Despite her epic awesomeness being sorely understated in this fresh-from-bed photo, here, nonetheless, is the ever-stunning Tilda Swinton.

Angelina Jolie with the kids. Thanks for all you do, Momma.

Dog the Bounty Hunter plays chicken with another sick puppy and, I have a feelin', somebody's goin' back to the pen.

At first this gentlerooster appeared to be Herbert (the creepy old man from Family Guy), then the karmic reality of Colonel Sanders came into focus... Somebody is lookin' extra crispy.

Marylin Manson on the cross again.

25

Richard Moll. It's difficult to tell from this photo, but he's 6 feet, 8 inches tall.

Charles Manson at home.

PHOTO BY JOACHIM DIPPOLD
OF BURGENLAND, AUSTRIA

PHOTO BY DENISE DAWSON, NORTH VANCOUVER, B.C.

The captivating Macy Gray.

PHOTO BY JULIE ROUNTREE (TIDEVIEWBANTAMS.WEBS.COM)

When we first saw this photograph, we were certain this was dame Helen Mirren prepping for another red carpet while waiting for make-up to fix her feathers, but upon further inspection we found out that this is Uma. Not Uma Thurman, but Uma the rescue chicken. Her rescue and rehabilitation was a mother/daughter team effort. She was found by a Gustie* vegetarian on the side of the road. Because of her age, Uma was assumed to be off to the battery cages. Even though she was caked in chicken feces, was black and blue under what feathers she had, was bleeding from her nostrils, had a battered and broken wing, and was slightly de-beaked, she made it out alive in such beautiful form. Uma was given to another Gustie vegetarian who could care for her for life at her parents' hobby farm, where she soon began to exhibit nesting behavior and within a few weeks laid her first egg. While Uma remained a solitary hen for nearly a year, she has since adapted to the addition of other chickens that comprise a happy flock.

*a name Gustavus Adophus College students proudly call themselves.

The captivating Tina Turner.

PHOTO BY JULIE ROUNTREE (TIDEVIEWBANTAMS.WEBS.COM)

Glenn Close as Cruella DeVil.

PHOTO BY NEVADAASPCA.ORG

MANY THANKS TO KATIE WINKELMAN OF SARTELL, MN
FOR THIS WONDERFUL PHOTO AND STORY.

Here we have (in order) Ann Coulter, Bill O'Reilly and Sean Hannity. They were each spotted several times, but none of our cameras could manage to make it past their large empty mouths.

Knock knock?

Who's there?
Interrupting chicken.
Interrupting chi....
Bill Maher.

PHOTO BY whatwhat (WHATWHAT.CO.UK)

"Your breasts are enormous and the fullness of your figure surely must cause your fellow hens pause."

HENHOUSE **FORUM**

Dear HENHOUSE Forum,
Never in my wildest dreams did I think this would ever happen to me but here I sit, frantically brooding, and in dire need of your help.

I live in a modest henhouse with about a dozen other hens. They are all fine ladies, all of them Rhode Island Reds, which means the house can get pretty chaotic at times as you can well imagine! Anyway, I myself am a gorgeous Golden Comet and can say without pause that for all of my laying days I have always been—without exception—a brown egg-layer. My mother was a browner and her mother before her was a browner. Well, I am devastated to say in the last few weeks, my eggs have become gradually paler. Yesterday, I was shocked to discover that I am pushing out almost pure white stones! The other hens have taken to calling me "Miss California Whitey" and, besides the tacky peck in their tone, I'm not even from California! Won't you help?
Can't coop,
Miss Brown, Feeling Down

Dear Miss Brown,
First, allow me to commiserate. The worst summer I ever spent was a single week with six Rhode Island Reds in an urban Baltimore henhouse facing due south in August. You want to talk about drama? If it hadn't been for the drinky drinky cleaning woman who left the door wide open while filching eggs, I'd still be there.

At any rate, what you are going through is completely normal, dear. If you are a particularly fluent layer, it is typical in the

course of a laying season that the color will fade. In fact, it's a rare breed that holds consistent pigment throughout the season. Also, hanging out in the strong sun and high temperatures of summer can produce a fading effect for your shells. My advice would be to tell those reds it's not the color that matters, but the quantity.
No bawk talking,
HF

Dear HENHOUSE Forum,
I just moved into a well-ventilated wooden house along a small, tranquil stream. The humans who tend to the other hens and I are kind and soft-spoken. The rooster who roams the grounds presents something of a surprise from behind each afternoon, but that is not why I am writing to you.

From the first day that I came to live here, the other hens have made it clear in no uncertain terms that my job is to produce eggs. And they've gone on to insinuate that by my not producing eggs, I am somehow shirking my duties to the humans and am therefore passing added work onto them (I have not seen them increase their egg count to compensate for me, btw). I have

always been a lousy layer and, up until now, have never been made to feel inferior because of it. If it makes any difference, they are all mottled black Anconas (not the prettiest of dames, IMHO), and I am a Jersey Giant.
I have enclosed a picture of myself to help you.
Eggshausted,
In Ovum My Head

PHOTO BY VELVET SPARROW (JACKSHENHOUSE.COM)

Dear Ovum,
This is a challenging letter to answer without raising an immediate dustup of feathers, but I will try. Let me clarify a few things for you. Your housemates are, among other things, an Italian breed. As such, they may be prone to getting a bit pushy and somewhat intolerant of those whom they perceive as weak or unproductive. That being said, Anconas are prolific layers and quite popular with the roosters.

You, on the other hand, my fine black darling, are a very impressive Jersey Giant, gorgeous in every way. Your breasts are enormous and the fullness of your figure surely must cause your fellow hens pause. That being said, I loathe to remind you of

30

an unpleasant truth: unlike the layer breeds that surround you, you are what is commonly referred to — quite vulgarly, I might add — as a table breed. If you do not know what that means, then consider your ignorance a blissful gift from the chicken gods who roost in peace.

Suffice to say that there is nothing wrong with you, my dear. You may simply go along the rest of your life in utter peace, brushing off the pecks and scratches from those jealous Anconas until that fine early morning when your "kind and soft-spoken" human comes and whisks you away with his warm, flannel-dressed arms.
Eggnorance is bliss,
HF

"CRACKED CORN"

CHILDREN OF THE CRACKED CORN

Dear HENHOUSE Forum,
Can you settle a dispute between me and the other hens up in this squawk box? It's been 16 suns since we last saw Benny Wattlechops, the shared rooster, outside our enclosure. Needless to say, many of

the bantams around me are still quite distraught. One of them, Sylvia Lynne, was standing at the fence scratching on the ground when Benny was snatched up by a large bird of prey. According to Sylvia Lynn, she gave a cry for help, but Benny valiantly ordered her to run inside, save herself, and tell the rest of us to remain in hiding until the bird was far out of sight. Sylvia Lynn didn't say a word until the next day, and even then it was only when she was asked about it. We all think she is full of chicken scratch, but there I go meandering off topic as I am wont to do.

The point is, there's a disagreement now brewing over whether or not a man is needed in our yard at all. My opinion is an unequivocal "no." It's been months since we've seen any little yellow downy ones pecking around the yard, which is completely fine by me. The last thing I need in my life is another clutch of chicks with sirens crowding up under my fluff. The only reason I'd even consider bringing in another rooster might be to knock that utterly insufferable Miss Tamala down from her perch. She's become entirely too bossy since Benny flew the coop. But we are a democratic group and, as it stands, are still at a stalemate with the voting. Bebe

is the only holdout. That's just because she hasn't understood a word we've said since she got her head swiped at by the visiting night raccoon last month.
What the cluck,
No Boys Allowed

Dear No Boys,
It's true that unless you are interested in procreation (which it is clear you are not, but, may I ask, have you considered the parental desires of the other ladies of the house? Something to ponder over your morning scratches, I suggest) a rooster is not particularly crucial—unless you count "soaring eagle decoy" as a commodity.

As you have noticed in Miss Tamala, one of the brood inevitably takes on the crown of "head honchetta" when the token male goes on extended vacation. I suggest that, rather than taking a blind vote, you steer into a greater discussion of the pros and cons of having a rooster. Should you decide to give way to a rooster-less home for the time being, know that you can always find many eligible roosters at your local shelter or on craigslist.
All my breast,
HF ∎

POULTRY

IN

MOTION

"ALL THEY KNOW OF HATE

IS THAT IT COULDN'T
BEAT THE LOVE OUT OF ME."

—Andrea Gibson

" Take me into your heart like I was a saint,
and you were a face of forgiveness blooming in a valley destined to sink further.
Be a river with me.
Be the storm.
The bend in the path,
the front porch, the heat in the south -

be a boot full of banjo strings.
A fistful of written songs,
a mouthful of chocolate dust.
When they come to take us,
stab them between the eyes.
Do not take your hand from around mine. "

"Night fell

or

was pushed."

—BRENDAN CONSTANTINE

"I have had the wind knocked out of me, but never the hurricane."

—JEFFREY McDANIEL

37

DARWIN'S CHICKENS

By T. S. Davis
Asheville, NC

Goat and I spent that winter of 1978 working on the Christmas tree farm next door to his house on Gehrke Road in microscopic Agnew, Washington. His place sat on the bluff overlooking the Strait of Juan De Fuca, a few miles outside Port Angeles. He and his wife, Pat, let me crash there for a few months when I got laid off and the married woman I was seeing ditched me for her husband, after all the time I had put into our relationship, trying to steal her away from him. You do things expecting one result, but you get something else. I'll admit, it wasn't a proud or stellar time in my life.

In the evenings we'd be bone tired from bulldogging Christmas trees, so we'd sit around drinking beer and smoking pot and watching the bald eagle nest in the dead tree on the bluff. Goat had a spotting scope and we were doing a volunteer eagle head count for the U.S. Fish and Wildlife Service, but in the haze of the pot smoke we often forgot how many we'd counted.

We also had a spider nicknamed Darwin that captured our attention. Darwin had cast a large web outside the bay window using the light inside the house as bait for bugs. While we were stoned, we'd amuse ourselves by catching insects and tossing them into the web to watch Darwin at work. We'd time the spider to see how long it took Darwin to lasso the insect and tie it down. It was a real bug rodeo.

One day as we sat there, numb from some pot apparently laced with opium, according to Goat, he surprised me by telling me he had bought a whole chicken house full of chickens from one of his buddies. I thought he was crazy. "What are we gonna do with them?" I said. "That's way too many to eat!" He said, "No, dipstick, we're gonna have eggs."

I loved eggs. I had just learned how to poach them, not chickens, but eggs, and I loved that thin film of cooked white drooled over the yoke. So I was definitely down with the idea of free eggs.

Goat planned to put the chickens in the ramshackle coop that stood unused out back, after a little remodeling to make it coyote proof. So we replaced the chicken wire and got lights in it for heat and Goat bought some feed. The big day finally arrived. It was time to pick up the chickens.

Bear in mind, none of us knew squat about chickens, especially about how to move a whole bunch of them from one place to another. So to plan for the move, Goat and I got real stoned and had Pat drive us on the back roads over to Sequim to pick up the chickens. Goat brought along a dozen burlap bags and a ball of twine. He explained the plan to me on the way over.

"Now the way to transport a chicken," he said authoritatively, "is to put it in the burlap bag. It can't see anything so it thinks it's safe." That made a kind of convoluted sense to me, but the obvious big unanswered question was this: how do you get a chicken into a burlap bag?

"How do you get a chicken into a burlap bag?" I said.

"Well, me and my chicken farmer buddy will go in the coop real quiet like while they're all sitting on their roost. He says it's real easy to pick them up when it's dark and they're all relaxed in there and just slip them into the bags one at a time. They can't get away in the coop."

"One chicken to a bag?" I said.

"That's right," Goat answered, "And then we crack the coop door and pass the bags out to you, one by one. You tie a string around the neck of the bag and gently place the bag in the back of the truck. Can you handle it?"

Somehow it sounded reasonable. Must have been the pot.

When we got there, the plan started off just like Goat had predicted. As he and his buddy slipped into the coop with the bags, Pat and I waited, short lengths of twine in hand. At first, all we heard from inside the coop was Goat whispering to his buddy and the chickens voicing soft coos and "bucks." That is, until Goat lunged at one of them.

From inside the dark coop was a cacophony of "Bwwwaaakkk!!! Buck! Buck! Buck! Buck! Bwwwaaakkk!!! Bwwwaaakkk!!!" and Goat yelling at his buddy to hold the bag open. A moment later, Goat cracked the door and thrust out a bag full of squirming squalling fowl. I roped it off and set

it in the truck.

It was then we all discovered what Goat and the chicken farmer had neglected to do – close the chicken door from the coop to the run. A dozen hens and two roosters had wisely escaped into the run where pandemonium now ensued. They ran in all four directions and took short hopping flights across the run and the frantic squalling was intense. From their point of view, the terrorists had arrived.

We were left with only one option — to try to catch each chicken while it ran from us. Pat and I joined the fun. Seriously, have you ever tried to catch a truly panicked chicken? Their evasive maneuvers would confuse a cruise missile. More than once I lunged too quickly and went down into a pile of chicken squirt trying to snatch a hen off the ground. What was worse was when I finally caught one, flapping and squawking and pecking, and tried to figure out how to hold onto it. Even after I secured it, then what? Oh yeah, holding it with one hand, gently slip it into the burlap bag, as Goat had admonished. Like trying to thread a live snake into a jar.

Eventually, all the chickens were cornered and caught and bagged and paid for, and we headed for the home coop back in Agnew. Amazing how easily they came out of the bags and took up residence with aplomb. Goat and I would smoke a bowl and go out to feed the chickens, which was really just an excuse to stand there, stoned and totally amused by the strutting roosters and unflappable hens acting out the inane drama of their existence. A real domesticated circus. Stoned or not, if you watch chickens long enough, they make you laugh.

Before long, the pecking order had been re-established, and there were fresh eggs for breakfast. The coyotes never got into the coop or the run. But what we really hadn't counted on, perched on top of the food chain in the dead tree, was the hungry bald eagle. It was like we were tossing bugs into a spider web.

Darwin, the real Darwin, would have been amused.

JANET RENO
By Stephen Snook

"I should take up jogging or modern dance," thought Janet Reno. She was trying to remember the last time she could fly. She enjoyed being airborne, but it had been quite some time, maybe even years. It was a fact that she was large for a chicken and, in an effort to move very quickly or run, she had to all at once give her legs forward and flap her wings with tremendous vigor. Expression set and determined, balance in question, Janet Reno would move in this manner across open spaces in the garden, halted over and over by the same tall vegetation, which always arrived as a surprise. Janet Reno understood that her ungainly and disruptive motions unsettled the other hens, but she also believed, or certainly entertained the idea, that one day she would again take flight and dive bomb the whole upper pecking order with heavy loaded droppings and clucky cackles of glee.

The sun was directly above, and the day was directly ahead. Janet Reno had just finished a dust bath, then a quick six-second surprise romp with the rooster, Marc Anthony. It was during those six-seconds that Janet Reno considered jogging or dance, but mostly she imagined herself in flight. Had she not been fresh from a dust bath, any observer would have noticed the sunlight glinting off her lovely plumage, tans and browns with streaks of gold and great plum and coriander. But covered up with dust, she just came off as another fat brown hen with big eyes. She wanted to possess more snazzabilty, as it were. Snazzability most definitely escaped Janet Reno.

Janet Reno left the other hens sunbathing on a gravel path and snuck back into the vegetable garden to snack on some spinach. The man who managed the entire goings-on at this farm had already chased her from the garden three or twelve times that morning, but Janet Reno enjoyed an entirely selective memory and regarded the vegetable garden as a chicken-friendly destination. Spinach and cabbage were her favorites. She consumed them often. Blissful as any hen might hope to be, Janet Reno moved off the spinach plants and headed to the pond for some water. Instead of goldfish staring back at her, that day the pond rapidly rose up the reflection of an American Bald Eagle.

It was sudden and absolute, without comprehension or understanding. Janet Reno was airborne, at last, held firmly in an eagle's talons by the edges of her wings, right where they joined her back. Janet Reno could see everything; hens running for cover, the man running and waving at her, the ponds, the garden, the hen house, the big hen house, the oh-so-wonderful everything. How happy happy happy. Happy Janet Reno. She was much higher than she had ever been before when she produced a most visceral clucky cackle and an incredibly accurately aimed, awfully soft and snazzy, loaded white dropping indeed.

PHOTO BY MICHELLE ROGERS, SONOMA, CA

WHY I HAVE DECIDED TO BECOME A CHICKEN KEEPER

By Laura Brown-Lavoie

The children had razor blades to sharpen their pencils, and suddenly I realized that each child in the class was holding a razor blade! But they would never have cut one another, whereas I saw weapons. What is it in certain imaginations that transforms a tool into a weapon? This body, which I am learning to sharpen.

"What bond have I made with the earth, having worn myself against it?" Unearthed like a stone, I was born uncut. Of course, there is a razor blade where my mother's arm meets her torso. But at Home Depot a woman should do-it-herself. Gathering tools, carving calluses into her fingers until her hands are tools too, and the line between object and body grows so blurry that if one becomes a weapon the other will too. Our bodies are not weapons, yet, day after day we place seeds in little cups of soil and coax them upwards.

So, it is decided, we will have chickens this year. Not because they are "easier than a dog, but harder than a cat," or for the omelets, but because many towns this morning are underwater and there is no way of knowing why mine is not.

The tectonics of this planet throw me, flailing, into the arms of my beloveds. Yes, on my map there is a pushpin with a heartbeat. Close to the epicenter. And in many other distant cities, a piece of yarn tied to each one, radiating out from Here. Or I am the epicenter, I, unraveled outwards, unknit by my longing to gather everyone close to me. But under those conditions I cannot write.

I ask myself: will you still be a writer after your town is swept away? And the response is the difference between using a razorblade to sharpen a pencil and using it to threaten my neighbors when all of us are hungry and only some of us have food. Will you still write despite the radiation that inevitably inches towards you?

The tectonics of this planet throw me to my knees and while I'm down there I might as well grow something. What bond have I made with the earth? It gapes. I imagine thousands of people falling into its maw.

So I have decided to look at my chickens from several angles, but to start from delight — from the totally nonsensical joy of a chick in a cardboard box in my bathroom — and to radiate out from there. To know that I will love it enough to build it a good coop, enough to feed it well, to keep it warm in the winter. That I will love it enough to keep feeding it even after it stops laying.

Today there is bread in the oven and boxes of seeds in my bedroom. I will be a chicken keeper because this year all of my tools still feel like tools in my hands. I will not wait for everything I own to turn into a weapon before I decide to use it.

PHOTO BY GEORGE SLATIN, NEW YORK CITY, NY

FROM SCRATCH

(The A-to-Z look at raising chicks from start to finish)

A.

Clear your schedule.

B Enlist someone mindful to help on days you must be away.

C Begin making one consistent sound the babies will come to know and recognize as you. I make a fast water drip sound. Chicks love constant feedback and the comfort your presence offers. Hold them warmly.

D They will nod off to sleep frequently. Let them rest and live in a large open/ventilated containment filled, at least one-inch thick, with pine shavings/absorbent bedding. Do not use newspaper (slippery surface can lead to "splayed leg") or cedar (aromatic oils irritate their lungs and can lead to respiratory issues). A storage bin that allows for repeated, thorough washing works well. They will live here for the next four to five weeks (provide at least two square feet per bird; the bigger the better). If using cardboard, consider implementing a removable liner. If you have an empty room with a wood floor that you can cover with bedding (and sneak in some outside dirt), you are very lucky.

E Keep the heat lamp plugged in. Chicks need to stay warm at 95 degrees Fahrenheit the first week, then 90 degrees Fahrenheit the second week, and so on. Be flexible. It's easy to regulate the temperature when your 250-watt bulb is housed in a brooder lamp with a clamp. Just gradually raise the lamp each week, or lower it when necessary.

F Observe behavior. If the chicks are distancing themselves from one another and the heat source, then it's too hot. If they're bunching up together directly under it, it's too cold. They should be at ease in all areas of the containment.

G Signs of good health: shiny eyes, clean face, smooth leg scales, alert and cautious, and — as they grow — their feathers will be shiny and their combs will be bright. Their beaks should be without overbite.

H Stay aware of possible lice/mites by checking the skin under their down feathers thoroughly for tiny black, red or tan bugs. If the chick's droppings cake up and block their vent opening, this can be fatal and is called "pasting up." Clean with warm water and a washcloth immediately (dip the chick's rear in warm water to loosen if very thick; be thorough), blow dry with your hand close to the chick's skin to ensure no overheating, then return the chick to the heat lamp.

I Handle chicks often (you'll be glad you did when they're older). Check in for a few minutes, then get them right back under the lamp.

J They'll drink from a "chick waterer," which eliminates potential drowning in a household dish and lessens the shavings/poop they con-stantly add by accident. Change their water frequently — if you wouldn't drink from it, neither should they.

K They'll eat from a "chick feeder," which also spares the constant introduction of mess. "Starter feed" contains all the nutrients a chick needs to thrive. Give them as much as they want, making it available 24/7.

L Chicks (and chickens) don't have teeth. They store "grit" (tiny stones) in their crop, which helps them to grind down the food they eat. Sprinkle plenty of grit on their food, or offer it in a separate chick feeder.

M Chickens absolutely love and prefer to roost on a perch. After the first week, introduce about a half-inch-in-diameter rod, fitted from one end of the chicks' box to the other. You'll all be pleased with this add-on.

N If everything in your house is in close prox-imity, and the chicks are making a stressed or siren-like noise at night, turn off the T.V. and be quiet. Now stay that way. Unlike many humans, chickens actually listen to their body's demand for sleep. This is a good time for you to adopt a healthy sleep schedule.

O If you're only raising one chick, and she's calling for you in sometimes alarming, manic chirps, she is likely lonely, missing you, looking for your company, and using her locater chirp on max volume. If you've left her to wander outside of her heat source too long, get her back to it pronto. If you're raising two or more at once, the chirping can still be a constant, but — because they comfort one another — far quieter.

P If the chick is incessantly calling out for your attention then running away when you approach, try seeing it from her instincts (i.e. sit down, be still and let her pick a spot to warm up under).

Q. If a chick is at ease on your shoulder or chest, wear a bib... it's not personal.

PHOTOS BY JAMES DOBSON (PEAKDISTRICTONLINE.CO.UK)

R On top of growing fast, chicks will also quickly learn to fly out of their box. A safe cover screen in which they cannot get hung or tangled may be your answer for keeping them safe in their enclosure at night.

S After a couple weeks, take them outside to a sunny, contained space in the grass (with shade and refreshments available), and let them scratch around. Chickens forage by scratching with their claws and pecking with their beaks upwards of 10,000 times per day.[6] Chicks dig it when you scratch too. See if you can contribute a tasty beetle already! Don't leave them unattended. They're especially susceptible to predators. They'll begin chirping loudly if they get too cold and want to go inside.

T Make sure your plans for transferring the chicks to a chicken coop are already in place. Consider the coop a macrocosm of what you've already successfully provided. The coop will have plenty of space, a heat lamp for cold weather, ventilation, a waterer, a feeder, grown-up poultry feed (they'll get their grit from scratching around now, but it's still a good idea to offer them a dish of this essential stuff), staggered perches (if needing more than one; so they don't drop bombs on each other), nest boxes with bedding, and HENHOUSE art for the walls. Make sure the place is free of any toxic paint or pest-dusting fumes. Have cracked corn and sunflower seeds at the ready for snack time. Hang a cabbage from a string and let 'em have some fun.

U To deter rodents, raise the chicken food off the ground in feeders with small outputs (as opposed to giant dishes that can feed the whole underground neighborhood). Keep all the extra feed in tightly lidded containers that can't be eaten through by rats.

V CONGRATULATIONS! Your chicks are ready to move outside permanently at around four to five weeks old (though their feathers will likely not be fully filled in until about eight weeks).

W Laying eggs takes its toll, draining calcium from a hens' body. The comb, wattles, ear lobes and legs will fade as calcium leaches out. Replenish them with feed containing calcium, supplements such as oyster shell, plenty of outdoor access to calcium-rich soil, and dried eggshells.

X The girls will love their privacy in the nest box. Cutting some curtains out of a burlap sack or an old sheet and attaching it with heavy-duty staples is very much appreciated and sure cuts down on henhouse drama. But don't worry about creating one box for every hen — the ladies don't mind sharing. Often, four or five hens will pick one "favorite" box for preferred laying.

Y Don't worry about combining different breeds and sizes of hens. They'll adapt just fine.

Z REVIEW: Initial shopping list (all of these items are relatively inexpensive):

- Large contained space (e.g. plastic storage bin, or box with liner)
- 250-watt infrared splash-proof heat bulb
- Pine wood shavings
- Heat reflector or "brooder" lamp with clamp and guard
- Chick waterer
- Chick feeder
- Starter feed
- Grit
- One-inch dowel or rod for perch
- Screen or mesh to place over the containment at night

LEEANN DUNN (URBANCHICKENSLIVINTHEDREAM.BLOGSPOT.COM)

PHOTO BY MICHAEL FILIPPONE OF FT. LAUDERDALE, FL WHOSE DREAM IS TO START A ROOSTER RESCUE SANCTUARY. IF YOU LIVE NEAR MICHAEL AND WANT TO HELP, CONTACT: MYLO36@AOL.COM

How NOT to Raise Chickens

A field guide for urban poultry farmers

Department of Waste Reduction   **Published: June 2011**

WARNING

Raising chickens is a commitment, not a fad!

There used to be a time when chickens were a common sight in American backyards. Although it is starting to become popular again, for the most part, most people don't raise their own livestock. Why not? It's hard work!

Remember, chickens aren't carrots: we're dealing with real living things here that need consistent, long-term care. Otherwise it's just another form of animal oppression.

If you're the kind of person that likes to wash dishes by hand and weave your own fabric, maybe raising chickens is for you.

Otherwise, please stick with tofu. Thanks!

JUNE 2011
www.firstcultural.com

chicken.firstcultural.com

51

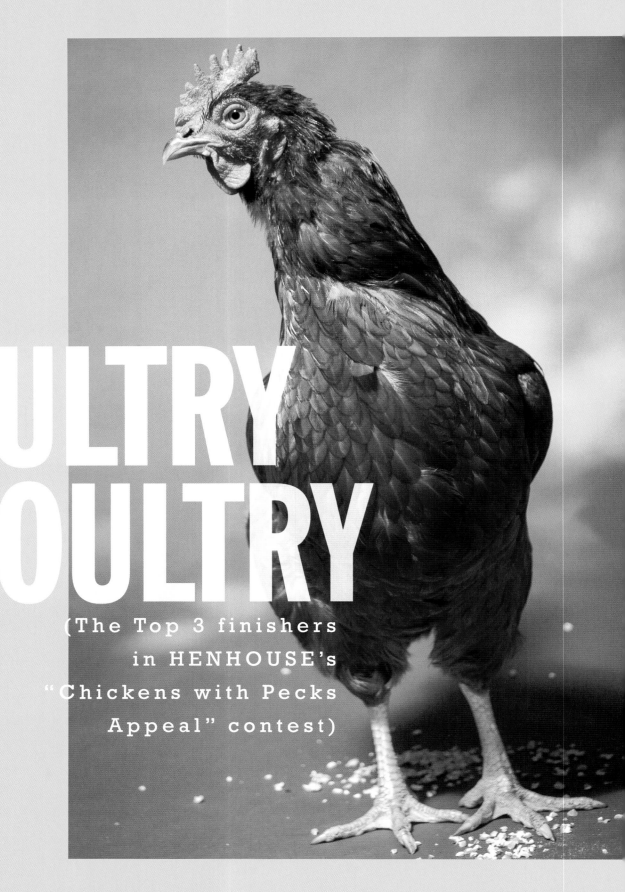

SULTRY POULTRY

(The Top 3 finishers in HENHOUSE's "Chickens with Pecks Appeal" contest)

WINGS

01

Sybil Fix is the keeper of this gorgeous, trim Rhode Island Red named "Wings." Born in the fall of 2008 (Charleston, SC), Wings is that eager first face in the coop window every morning, geared up and ready to get moving on a textured day of free rangin', sun-soakin' and bok bok'ing around. Named Wings for how much she enjoys stretching full-out to show off her feathers, she's quite the character, known on the grounds as curious class clown, tenacious socialite and athletic as all get out. Her turn-offs are people who eat chicken wings (especially in buckets), listening to the band Rush and being cooped up even one minute longer than necessary. Always the last to come in for bedtime, never leave out your art supplies if Wings is visiting; she's got a real taste for oil sticks.

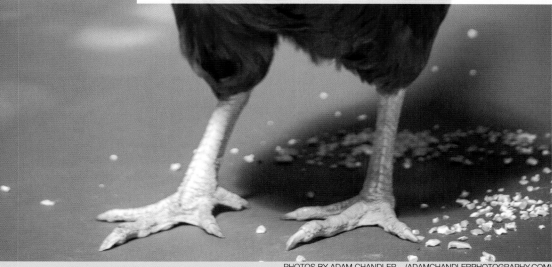

PHOTOS BY ADAM CHANDLER   (ADAMCHANDLERPHOTOGRAPHY.COM)

53

02

MEET LIESEL

Meet Liesel. Liesel is a Buff Orpington weighing in at two pounds of bless-her-little-heart. She loves scrumptious corn tortillas, taunting dogs and being carried around by the people. She doesn't mind tagging along for a walk to burn off those compost pile calories either. Eating any and all kale found in the garden is something she does a little too well. Liesel, behave!

When we put out the call for Sultry Poultry, we expected a couple cocky roosters to submit a colorful tail feather or two for consideration, but we certainly didn't expect this exquisite gentleman.

MEET BEAUREGARD

of Fair Oaks, CA. When not grooming the lawns on Main Street or helping elderly citizens cross the road (no reason), you can find Beauregard kindly tending to a fine flock of mild-mannered hens around town, treating them to adventurous outings through a polite and generous community.

Beauregard the Silver Sebright.
Eat your heart out, hens, and take
a couple notes while you're at it.

COOPS!
- THERE IT IS -
COOLEST COOPS THIS SIDE of the MISSISSIPPI

Keeping chickens requires that you have a place to keep them. That place can be built into almost anything as long as a few important housing requirements are met. I would like to build a chicken coop that looks just like a flying saucer of 1960's sci-fi vintage. Imagine a hovering silver craft with that iconic dome window on top. Every morning when I set out to let the chickens down the hydraulic ramp that drops from the bottom, I would get to watch them bob up and down in that dome window, excited to see me come to set them free for the day. I just know it would make me laugh, out loud, each and every time. The point is, get creative with your hen house, and have fun, because this is the fun part, and besides, a chicken house is a must have. A "Chicken Ranch" is another thing entirely.

There are basically two types of coops. Portable coops (also known as chicken tractors), and fixed coops. The tractors are best for larger spaces where the coop can be moved over the landscape, giving the chickens protection from predators while they move around the property eating bugs, grass and seeds. The tractor-style coop provides a great way to fertilize your yard and feed your chickens. A permanent coop, a traditional chicken house with an attached wire run, is designed to remain fixed in

place. This is best for backyard chickens if you have a limited amount of space.

It's important to consider a chicken's needs when buying or building a chicken coop. Proper ventilation is very important to chicken health but a coop must also protect from the elements. Roost and nesting box space, light, and predator protection all need to be designed into a functional and healthy habitat. Each chicken will require three to four square feet of space, double this for the run. Nesting boxes should be 15"x15"x12" and if you drape the front with sack cloth or burlap this will provide a laying chicken with the privacy a girl needs.

Chicken houses can be made from so many things that may otherwise be sitting empty or unused. Revamp an old shed, boathouse, camper or fifth wheel trailer. Create a coop from some old scrap lumber; build one from stones, barrels, or tires. A good imagination and an eye for style are your best tools if building your own. Here are some coops to inspire, teach and taunt you with all the possibilities that a simple chicken coop can be, so take inventory of your skills, your materials, and your imagination in order that you might build the chicken coop of your dreams.

TRACTOR STYLE

This, The Gothic Ark, is a take on the centuries-old English Ark design. It is basically a chicken tractor and a coop in one, and is designed to move around the yard so the hens can eat the grasses underneath the coop. Standard size is four feet by eight feet and holds four hens.

FIXED

A custom gothic plank coop

Green Frog Designs of the UK produce these fantastic innovative coops. They are made entirely of recycled industrial waste plastic, designed and cut into sheets for easy assembly. These coops won't rot, fade or easily weather, plus you can clean them out with a water hose and they'll dry fast! Green Frog Designs is a U.K. company looking for a U.S. manufacturer. If anybody out there is interested in partnering, holler at 'em.

The Chicken wagon is ideal for up to 6 larger birds or 12 bantams. There are two individual nest boxes, each with a rollaway nest box insert, which helps keep eggs clean. Once laid, the eggs roll backwards into a collecting area, which is covered by a flap. Easy access to the collecting area is provided by a lockable sliding cover at the rear of the house. The nest boxes can be easily removed, if required. Access to inspect the birds and for cleaning is via a full-height front door which can be quickly opened, yet securely fastened in just a few seconds. Easy access makes regular cleaning a breeze.

Or check out these small house designed to accommodate 2-3 birds, with adjustable vent dials on the side. A handy handle on the roof opens and closes the swing door.

Two coops by
Sparrow & Finch

The Priory Hen House
(above) is perfect for someone with a small garden who still wants a few hens. Big enough for five bantams or three large hens, the traditional beehive shape will look stunning in any setting.

The Babbington
For those who want the look and feel of five-star-hotel luxury, the beautiful Babington Hen House is perfect. Based on a Sussex barn, the Babington is small enough for the back garden hen keeper, but still easily accommodates up to 8 large chickens or 12 bantams. Designed and built by Sparrow & Finch.

Green Chicken Coop

Dan Cohen of Green Chicken Coop (greenchickencoop.com) designs and builds coops out of wood from timber plantations that are certified to be ecologically sustainable. The plywood used is exterior grade, 3/4 inch thick, from certified managed forests and free from any harmful glues or chemicals. The cedar shake roof shingles and underlayment protect the house from most weather conditions and the "environmentally friendly" paint is non-toxic, exterior latex with a low-VOC as well as a low-VOC colorant.

ELIZABETH

"Elizabeth" house with a 15-foot enclosed run (and Dan offers an option to put it on wheels!)

Shiloh Pottery, Inc. built this outstanding Hansel and Gretel fixed coop with gorgeous round door and matching dormer window. Scalloped roof overhang and vertical siding trim help give this house such a warm, inviting style. The run is attached to the side.

PHOTO BY MARTY AND KEN HANKINS (SHILOHPOTTERY@HOTMAIL.COM)

John Wright, an architect in Portland, Oregon created this fantastic familiar-looking coop. Stylish, attractive and practical with just the right amount of rough-around-the-edges, it's portable and made of recycled cedar. The roof is fiberglass so light may pass through, but a metal roof is optional. The nesting boxes have exterior access, and the slatted siding provides ventilation. Lookin' so much like the Winnebago camper van of the seventies, just adorn with bumper stickers and enjoy. "I try to push the fact that I do other stuff," says John, referring to his architecture projects for humans (wrightdesignoffice.com), "but everyone wants to talk about the chicken coops." Understandably so!

PHOTO BY JOHN WRIGHT (MODERNCOOP.COM)

WOODEN WONDERS

Features on this intriguing hobbit hole hen house include hinged front and rear windows, a ridge vent for plenty of ventilation, and a rear access door to the nest boxes.

Berg Danielson,

a carpenter in Seattle Washington, started building chicken coops in response to the slowing economy and downturn in house building. The result, Saltbox Designs (SaltboxDesigns.com), builds some of our favorite hen houses. Berg's designs are a mix of country quaint and modern convenience. He constructs his houses of western red cedar, the bulk of it recycled or salvaged from scrap. The look is simple and clean and perfect for the backyard chicken.

A built-in herb and flower box shades the small run under this Saltbox design.

This Saltbox coop is designed to house seven laying hens. Two nesting boxes are accessed from the smaller door beneath the shed roof, at a nice comfortable height for easy egg collection. The interior features an upper roost, nesting boxes, and space for an optional feeder and waterer. A ladder extends to the ground and raises up by pulling a cord, keeping the birds safe from predators and rodents during the night. Wheels on the back legs keep the coop easy to move about the property.

Below, a large run is attached to the above Saltbox design. A concrete border keeps the white shavings out of the grass and neatly contains the chicken area.

BACKYARD
COOP

One of your first steps toward keeping chickens is to make them a home. Depending on price and taste, coops range from simple enclosures to poultry Taj Mahals. The plans shown here offer directions for building a quality, affordable coop that you and your birds can love.

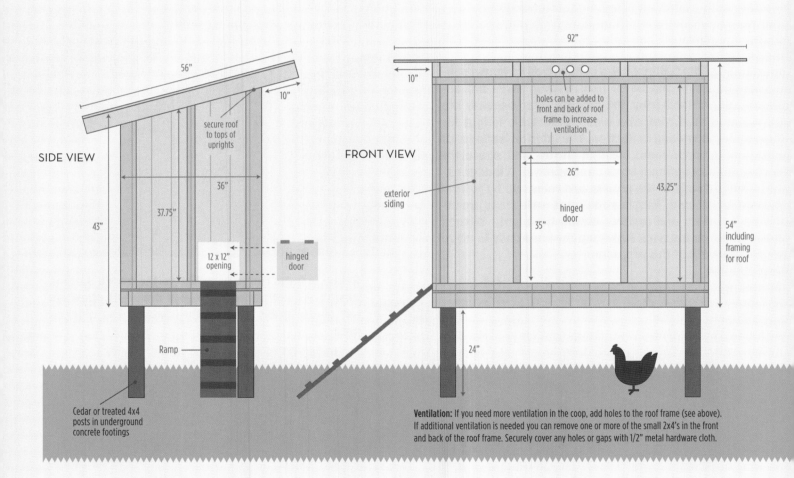

SIDE VIEW

56"
10"
secure roof to tops of uprights
36"
37.75"
43"
12 x 12" opening
hinged door
Ramp
Cedar or treated 4x4 posts in underground concrete footings

FRONT VIEW

92"
10"
holes can be added to front and back of roof frame to increase ventilation
exterior siding
26"
43.25"
hinged door
35"
54" including framing for roof
24"

Ventilation: If you need more ventilation in the coop, add holes to the roof frame (see above). If additional ventilation is needed you can remove one or more of the small 2x4's in the front and back of the roof frame. Securely cover any holes or gaps with 1/2" metal hardware cloth.

Before you begin building, we urge you to do your own research, get extra help, and modify these plans as needed. Also, have big fun.

STEPS

The following steps provide a broad outline of how to construct your coop. If you're new to building, familiarize yourself with basic methods of framing the floors, walls and roof before you get started. Your local hardware store can be a good resource.

1 Start with the four posts, anchoring them underground with concrete footings (see floor framing detail for measuring the placement of each post). Then frame the floor and attach the 72" x 36" sheet of 3/4 plywood to the floor frame.

18 SQUARE FEET

INTERIOR OF COOP | 3 TO 5 LAYING HENS | ABOUT 12 EGGS PER WEEK

TOOLS

ear plugs

Additional tools may be necessary. Always use power tools with major caution.

MATERIALS

GENERAL
galvanized wood screws
(4) galvanized door hinges
(2) door latches
(1) board for ramp
(5-6) 1 x 2 boards for ramp "steps"
(4) 4 x 4 treated or cedar posts- 36"
(4) concrete footings

Siding material - Use 1/2" plywood or ask your local hardware store for additional options.

FLOOR ASSEMBLY
(4) 2 x 4 - 33"
(2) 2 x 4 - 72"
(1) 3/4 plywood - 72" x 36"

WALLS ASSEMBLY
(6) 2 x 4 - 43.25" (front wall)
(1) 2 x 4 - 26" (front wall)
(4) 2 x 4 - 72" (front & back)
(6) 2 x 4 - 32.25" (back wall)
(2) 2 x 4 - 37.75" (side walls)

ROOF ASSEMBLY
(4) 2 x 4 - 56"
(4) 2 x 4 - 18"
(2) 2 x 4 - 26"
(1) 1/2 plywood - 92" x 56"

Roofing material - 92" x 56" Options include corrugated roofing, composite three-tab shingles, and more.

FLOOR FRAMING

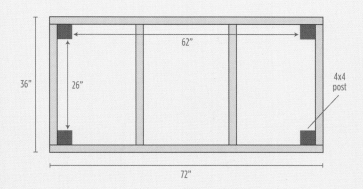

62"
36"
26"
4x4 post
72"

ROOF FRAMING

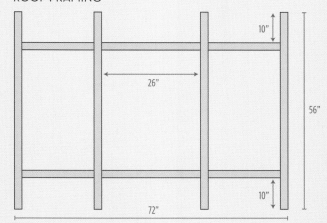

10"
26"
56"
10"
72"

TIME & COST

Yes, it will take resources to build your coop. But don't feel discouraged. If your friends or family are handy with tools, hit them up for help. And you can save significant money by using salvaged materials.

APPROXIMATE COST:
$300 OR LESS

APPROXIMATE BUILD TIME:
3-4 DAYS

2 Attach 2x4's flat on the plywood floor, flush with the floor's outer edge (see front view detail). Then attach the four corner uprights (two 2x4's per upright). Next, frame the remainder of the walls, following the front view detail for measurements of the front door frame.

3 The roof may be built separately and completed then raised onto the coop and attached at each upright. Last, attach the siding, install the hinged doors and the ramp, and apply stain or paint to the exterior.

GOOD TO KNOW:

• all dimension lumber is 2x4 unless otherwise indicated.

• one nesting box should accommodate 3-5 hens. Try attaching a wooden vegetable crate or other sturdy box in a corner, about 6-12"off the floor. Add extra nesting boxes if needed.

• to provide inexpensive perches for nocturnal roosting, attach several sturdy natural branches across a corner of the coop.

Illustration and plans by Tim Sanders (TimSandersDesign.com), based on the work of Lyanda Lynn Haupt (LyandaLynnHaupt.com; TheTangledNest.com) and family.

HENS GONE ~~WILD~~

What All That Chicken Racket Really Means

When I first began keeping company with these energetic creatures, I couldn't help but tune-in to their verbal cues. At first, it all sounded like a whirl of random announcements like, "We're gonna ransack your garden, Bud!" or "I'm gonna scratch this dirt, y'all!" or "How did you get on that side of the fence with all this fence in the way?!" and "Let's meet on the porch and poop together! Woot Woot!" Soon, I realized I was just projecting.

Bring to mind the most common chicken impersoation (bwawk bawk bawk bawk bagaawk!). It's a pretty accurate impression called a "cackle" ("to give a raucous, clucking cry;" thank you, Google dictionary).

A cackle seems to be the go-to line for chickens when announcing most anything. The cackle varies in resonance depending on what's being announced. Often, it appears she's just announcing, "Ladies and gentleman around the world, I've laid an egg! I have laid an egg! I have laid an egg! I've laid an egg! I've laid an egg. I've laid an egg--" Until she's good and ready to stop announcing that she has, in fact, laid an egg. While many folks believe this to be her way of letting others know she is a productive member of the community, some believe she is likely saying, "Thank goodness that's over! Who wants to hit the calcium with me?!"

Dr. Erich Baeumer of Wiedenau, Germany believes the cackle following an egg lay dates back to when hens in the wild would lay in hidden nests. After each delivery, the hen would cackle to regain contact with the rest of the flock. Dr. Baeumer has studied chickens since 1954, when he began working with Professor Erich von Hoist at the Institute of Behavior Physiology near Munich. Chickens were repeatedly and extensively photographed and recorded. After documenting hours of chickens talking, Dr. Baeumer was able to select clearcut examples of chicken "sentences" that could be related to the photographs and records of specific chicken actions. He confirms that chicken language is internationally consistent.

In a report released by The Humane

PHOTO BY CAMILLE SHEPPARD DOHRN   (CAMELLIABLOSSOMS.COM)

Society regarding communication skills among chickens, they explain, "Communication begins prior to hatching. Embryos emit a distress call, when cold, for example, and the hen responds to such calls by moving the egg in the nest. Developing chicks also emit pleasure calls when the hen responds... Nest mates also influence each other with their vocalizations. Clicking and bill clapping sounds made during late development are thought to help synchronize hatching, so that all the chicks in a clutch break free of their shells at approximately the same time."

Chickens develop a diverse catalog of vocal signals. Young chicks display 12 different types of intentional calls, and 19 additional calls have been identified for adult fowl. Adult chickens have two distinct alarm calls, or cackles: one for aerial predators, the other for predators on the ground. The alpha male call to warn of an aerial predator "omit[s] the conspicuous broadband pulse at the beginning of an aerial alarm call after the first in a series, and selectively retain[s] the more cryptic tonal element in those that follow." This warns those whom the caller intends to warn, while allowing the caller to take cover as quietly as possible. For ground predators, males will often give a high-pitch siren. It says, "Y'all, something with teeth and bad manners is walking towards us. Scatter in such-and-such fashion."

Research done on acoustic communication in chickens by Anne Wignall of Macquarie University in Australia reports, "My research asked whether chickens also have an 'all-clear' signal that tells conspecifics it is safe to return to normal activity such as feeding. This project discovered that while chickens do have an 'all-clear' signal, it is non-specific. This means that any call that is not an alarm call (e.g. crowing, food calls) can serve as an 'all-clear' signal."

When the chickens and I first arrived in each other's lives, I couldn't tell if they were griping or grateful. Here's some of what I came to understand in Pacific Northwest vernacular (Kidding. While pitch, tone, and human interpretation of spelling greatly vary, chicken language is thought to be consistent all over the world):

"Bu-bu-bu-bu-buhhh" *means,*
"Hello, let's do this!"

The soft lilting question,
"Huh-nnnnnnn?" *means what it sounds like,*
"What are you doing?" *Sometimes it sounds to me like a door, cautiously creaking open.*

[In a deep, greedy tone]
"Ooon-hwaah" *is usually geared toward other chickens, stating,* **"Outta my way, Sister, I want your space."**

"Cuc-cuc-cuc-cuc" *warns of things like,* **"There's a baby raccoon checkin' us out. Be ready."**

"Look-a-look-a-look-a-look" *is saying,* **"My, it's a beautiful day. Y'all wanna stroll the yard for sweet dustbathin' spots?"**

[In a rich cautioning tone]
"Kwaark kwaark kwaark" *says,* **"I'm in my nest box. Don't bother me."** *Hens are very protective when they're sitting on eggs.*

Roosters make a sound akin to "look, look, look" when they find food. It's an announcement to the ladies, but if the women already know of the food, they're not impressed. Along with "tidbitting" (a rooster's "check-out-my-goods dance"), a rooster will coo softly in an attempt to entice a hen. Regarding the common crow of a rooster (cock-a-doodle-doo!), he will sound it whenever he wants to, and for whatever reason he wants to. Our roosters have always crowed most in the morning and bedtime. If you don't have a rooster, you may have noticed how Miss Alpha Betty has already taken over and made herself known to the others. She is also the chief executor of alarm calls to warn against predators.

If you hear a loud hen squawk followed by a group kerfluffle, run toward your chickens fast. Something, like a predator, has likely surprised the whole crew. Whistle loudly and sharply to scare off whoever has disturbed your brood; this will especially work on a coyote (raccoons can be quite a bit more audacious). If you arrive to find the ruckus short lived, then they were likely just trying one another's patience. If the kerfluffle has translated to a loud repetitive group protest upon your arrival, and everyone is still very much on guard: first, remain aware of your entire surroundings, then do a head count.

You'll come to understand chickens well enough to realize that what you once thought sounded like just another "bawk!" now sounds exactly like "hawk!" (but as if the chicken had suddenly run into a speed bump, then consecutively bounced its chin off several, smaller follow-up bumps). If there's a chicken sound you're still not sure about, keep observing. Be patient. Watch after them well. Chicken language is consistent, so compare notes with friends.

Also, a little-known fact is that chickens have parroting abilities, so you can teach them new chicken sounds specifically designed for your household (no, not really, but if you were my little brother I would keep encouraging this until you actually tried it). ∎

In the ever-endearing Recipe For Raising Chickens *Minnie Rose Lovgreen explains the sounds a mother hen makes for her chicks. Here are some of Minnie's translations:*

*"The mother says, '**brrp, brrp, brrp... brrp, brrp, brrp,**' in a deep tone, and [the chicks] all come around her. Then she picks up a little food and drops it down."*

*"If the food is not good, she says, '**Krrrk,**' in a low tone, meaning, '**Don't touch it!**'"*

*"If the food is all right, she says, '**drrrp, drrrp, drrrp,**' in a higher pitch..."*

*"When there is danger of predators, the mother goes, '"**crrk, crrrk, crrrk,**"' in a low-pitched voice. The chicks all get under her or stand at attention."*

*Chicks "**peep, peep, peep**" when they're bothered (usually cold or locating others).*

*If a chick is terrified, a high-pitched siren goes, "**Trrr! Trrr! Trrr!**"*

PHOTO BY TRENTON BARNES AND JULI BOWEN   (OLIPHAUNTPHOTOGRAPHY.COM)

HENS

CHICKEN-LOVERS TURN tHE BIG GUNS ON HATCHERIES

(a.k.a. Eat My Scratch, USPS! Or... Why to Not Buy Chickens From Hatcheries, Feed Stores, or Via Airmail, EVER. Or... I'm Gon' Ruffle Your Feathers, Chicken Killah! Or... This is a Monster Cluck Rally.)

&

AMMO

No butterin' you up. No walkin' on eggshells. No sugar coats. No excuses. Know this:

* Most chickens are bought from hatcheries, or feed stores whose chicks come from hatcheries.

* Hatcheries ship those day-old chickens via the United States Postal Service without any legal oversight.

* Hatcheries also promote and sell those baby chicks as novelty holiday gifts.

* No food, water, comfort or compassionate provisions are offered throughout this shoddy three-day relocation.

* Hatcheries and the U.S. Postal Service have successfully lobbied Congress for permission to airmail newborn chicks as "perishable matter."

* Newborn chickens (along with geese, ducks, partridges, guinea fowl, pheasants, quails and turkeys) do not travel in weather-controlled, ventilated compartments like you, or as "cargo" like your dog and cat.

* Newborn chickens are flown with the mail in often freezing or blistering temperatures, enduring untold delays on and off the ground.

* This is the cheapest way for a hatchery to fly these sentient newborn babies to get used as dyed Easter gifts, science projects, breeding, cockfighting, target practice, or whatever the customer wants to do with them.

* Chicks who survive the costs of shipping and handling (physical and mental trauma, starvation and dehydration) are often sick, weak, dying or dead upon arrival.

* Unfortunately, buyers are often ignorant of how to properly and humanely care for the fragile little gals when they show up.

* "A day-old chick can no more withstand three days in a dark, crowded box than can any other newborn." — Dr. Jean Cypher, a veterinarian specializing in avian medicine.[7]

* Adopt. Breeding displaces existing animals who need homes.

* Half of the chicks hatched by hatcheries and commercial breeding facilities are male.[8]

* Since male chicks are of zero value in the production of eggs, a quarter billion per year are disposed of at the hatchery.[9]

* Once a chick's sex is determined (at one or two days old), unwanted males and deformed females are suffocated in the garbage, or ground up alive for fertilizer/feed, or sold for meat production.[10]

* Poultry is exempt from humane slaughter laws so there is nothing in place to protect chicks from these "cost-efficient" and cruel methods of disposal, except you.

THE CHICKEN INDUSTRY

PHOTOS AND TEXT REPRINTED WITH PERMISSIONS FROM
PEOPLE FOR THE ETHICAL TREATMENT OF ANIMALS (PETA.ORG).

BROILER CHICKENS

Virtually all chickens raised for their flesh (or "broiler chickens" as they are referred to by the meat industry), spend their lives crammed into massive, windowless sheds that typically hold as many as 40,000 birds each.

Chickens can function well in groups of up to about 90, a number low enough to allow each bird to find his or her spot in the pecking order. In crowded groups of thousands, however, no such social order is possible and, in their frustration, they relentlessly peck at each other, causing injury and death.

The intense confinement and extreme crowding on factory farms also results in unimaginable filth and disease. [Washington Post writer Peter Goodman], who visited a chicken shed, said that the "dust, feathers and ammonia choke the air in the chicken house and fans turn it into airborne sandpaper, rubbing skin raw."

Michael Specter, a longtime staff writer for The New Yorker, also visited a chicken shed and wrote, "I was almost knocked to the ground by the overpowering smell of feces and ammonia. My eyes burned and so did my lungs, and I could neither see nor breathe... There must have been 30,000 chickens sitting silently on the floor in front of me. They didn't move, didn't cluck. They were almost like statues of chickens, living in nearly total darkness, and they would spend every minute of their six-week lives that way."

These journalists could leave, but chickens are forced to breathe ammonia and particulate matter from feces and feathers all day long. Many suffer from chronic respiratory diseases, weakened immune systems, bronchitis, and "ammonia burn," a painful eye condition.[11]

A 2006 study by Consumer Reports found that a staggering 83 percent of grocery market chickens it tested were infected with either campylobacter or salmonella bacteria or both. The extremely high prevalence of dangerous contaminants in chicken flesh is due largely to the filthy conditions in the sheds where they are raised. On factory farms, they are fed large quantities of powerful antibiotics to keep them alive in conditions that would otherwise kill them: chickens are given nearly four times the amount of antibiotics as human beings or cattle in the U.S.[12]

Chickens are also genetically manipulated and regularly dosed with drugs to make them grow faster and larger. The average breast of an eight-week-old chicken is seven times heavier today than it was 25 years ago.[13] Because of this unnaturally accelerated weight gain, these very young birds frequently die of heart attacks and lung collapse, something that would almost never happen in nature. According to *Feedstuffs*, a meat-industry magazine, "Broilers now grow so rapidly that the heart and lungs are not developed well enough to support the remainder of the body, resulting in congestive heart failure and tremendous death losses".[14]

In addition, chickens on today's factory farms almost always become crippled because their legs cannot support the weight of their bodies. In fact, by the age of six weeks, 90 percent of broiler chickens are so obese that they can no longer walk. Many crippled chickens on factory farms die when they can no longer reach the water nozzles.[15]

BREEDER CHICKENS

The breeding animals who give birth to the eight billion broiler chickens killed in the U.S. each year have been referred to as Gallus Neglectedus, or "neglected chicken," by Dr. Joy Mench, a poultry scientist at the University of California, because their welfare is completely ignored. Like the broiler chickens to whom they give birth, breeder chickens are confined to filthy sheds without access to sunlight, fresh air, or anything else that they would enjoy in nature. When these birds are very young—usually just one to 10 days old—hot blades are used to cut large chunks off their sensitive beaks so that they won't peck each other out of frustration caused by the intense confinement. Sometimes their toes, spurs and combs are also cut off. The birds are not given any painkillers to

ease the agony of this mutilation, and many de-beaked chickens starve to death because they are in too much pain to eat.

Breeder chickens are forced to live on factory farms for more than a year. Because they live so much longer, they face an even higher risk of organ failure and death as they grow larger and larger because of their manipulated genetics. In an attempt to fix this problem, the industry drastically limits the feed given to breeding birds, keeping the animals in a constant state of hunger and frustration.

When the birds drink more water to try to relieve their hunger, factory farm operators often reduce the available drinking water so that they won't have to clean up wet manure.[16] Some farmers shove thin plastic rods through the delicate nasal cavities of male breeding birds. The rods stick out of both sides of their faces, preventing them from reaching through the wire barrier to eat the females' food. [Editor's note: the rods are primarily used to prevent cannibalism, typically, because the chicken is unable to focus and therefore will not successfully peck other birds when in such confinement.]

After more than a year of deprivation and confinement, the bodies of these breeding birds are too worn out to produce enough chicks for the farmer to sell. Frail and exhausted, they are loaded onto trucks and sent to slaughter.[17]

WHAT'S MORE *(from a separate factsheet by P.E.T.A. entitled, "Chickens Used For Food"):*

At the slaughterhouse, [chicken's] legs are forced into shackles, their throats are cut, and they are immersed in scalding-hot water to remove their feathers. Because they have no federal legal protection (birds are exempt from the Humane Methods of Slaughter Act), almost all chickens are still conscious when their throats are cut, and many are literally scalded to death in the feather-removal tanks after missing the throat cutter."

The Organic and Free Range Myth

ORGANIC [CHICKEN] PRODUCTS

We've all seen the grocery store packages of meat, eggs

and dairy products decorated with reassuring phrases such as "natural" and "free-range" and pictures of happy animals running around quaint country barns. But people who buy organic or free-range animal products because they think that the animals are treated well are sadly mistaken.

Many organic and free-range farms cram thousands of animals together in sheds or mud-filled lots to increase profits, just as factory farms do, and the animals often suffer through the same mutilations — such as debeaking, without painkillers — that occur on factory farms.

Organically raised chickens on some farms suffer from higher mortality rates than drugged chickens because extremely crowded, filthy housing conditions, coupled with a lack of antibiotics, can lead to even more parasites than are already found in drugged chickens.

A HEALTHIER ALTERNATIVE?

The only advantage that organic products have is that

they do not contain antibiotics, hormones, or arsenic-based additives (as many non-organic chicken products do). Many organic and free-range animals are killed in the same slaughterhouses as animals from factory farms, so their flesh is subject to the same potential for bacterial contamination from unsanitary conditions. ∎

Note from the editor: *Know your local farmers and their practices. While not all free-range/organic labeling is poppycock, ya gotta stay mindful of how big business has negatively manipulated positive words to suit their profits.*

HEN & THE ART

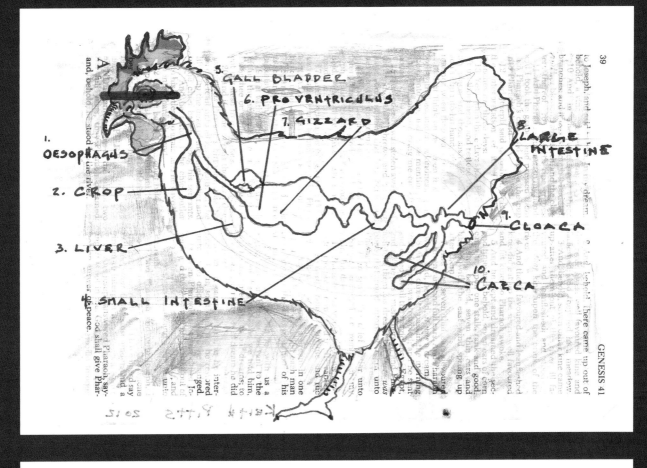

Hen
embroidered watercolors by Karen Grenfell (mimilove.net)

Family Farm

*Art by Jennifer Davis
(jenniferdavisart.com)*

Mother Hen

Rooster

Late

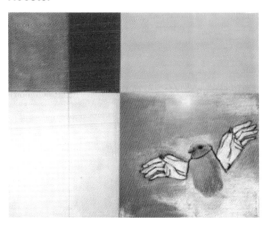

Apparatus

Source

Rooster Earth

False-Hearted Chicken
paper collage by Hollie Chastain (holliechastain.com)

"Hideaway"
By Danielle Pope, Victoria, B.C.

Oil on canvas
by Gustav Klimt courtesy of Awesome Art (info@awesome-art.biz)

FASHIONABLE

DOS & DON'TS

DO

KEEP IT SMOOV.

The massive staff here at HENHOUSE voted this gorgeous Golden Laced Wyandotte from Sonoma County, Marta Mannix, a fash-hen "DO" for her ability to "keep it smoov." Everyone knows fashion is all about attitude, and here at HENHOUSE Headquarters we likes to keep it smoov.

Even after being entirely sat upon by Liesel (bottom left) in the nest box (hens can be so stubborn about sharing), and busted for eating her own eggs (chickens do this if introduced to the deliciousness via accidental breakage; doesn't anybody knock around here?), and wrongfully-ish accused of tagging the back fence, Marta remains as calm and rounded (indeed) as can be.

With her shiny, all-natural feathered hair (no, ladies, that is not a cream rinse) and that well-contained, full-figured figure, we can't help but feature this super starlet of chill. It sure was a stressful morning for this precious former pullet perch activist, but my goodness she wears it well.

When asked how she managed to keep it so smoov all the time, even under pressure, Marta cooly cooed, "Ain't no thang but a chicken wang."

DON'T

MIXED MESSAGES

Anybody wanna tell this stud that chickens don't go pee pee?

PHOTO BY ASHLEY KNIGHT
(ASHLEYKNIGHTPHOTOGRAPHY.COM)

DO

HANDLE WITH CARE

"Anyway, here's Alice in her apron/saddle."
– Username: Azygous

's not always fun or easy raising chick-
ns. Occasionally, one of our crew in-
roduces us to a brand new health
oncern to which we were previously
blivious. Our sweet and confident Ma-
an hen, Olive Juice, grew a raw bald
pot on her back right in the center just
bove the tail. I began reading forums
nd articles to see if I could be of im-
nediate assistance in alleviating any
iscomfort Olive may have been experi-
ncing. That's when I came across this
omewhat relative entry by Carol Rawle
f Trinidad, CO (username: Azygous on
ackyardChickens.com) regarding her
ttle friend, Alice:

Alice is a one-year-old [Silver Laced] Wyandotte who's bottom
f the pecking order. She's under-size because she waits for per-
ission to eat, and she gets pecked constantly.

think once the feathers get picked out, and the pinfeathers start
rowing in, it's irresistible to all of them, including the victim, to
ontinue to pick out the blood-rich pin feathers. This sets up a
ever-ending cycle resulting in [apparent] permanent baldness.

To give Alice a fighting chance, I made her an apron/saddle, and
ncluded shoulder ruffles because she was bald on her shoulders
s well. She's been wearing the saddle for several months now,
irt bathes, lays eggs, gets mated with by the roo, all wearing her
addle. It keeps her from getting sunburned while the feathers
loooooowly grow back, which is taking so long because she's
erpetually undernourished due to her place in the flock. I've tried
eeding her separately, but she refuses to eat except when with
he others. (She needs their permission, it appears.)"

HENHOUSE just had to include Carol's saddle apron with
our Fashion-Able DO's because it's practical, well-crafted
and completely re-shaping the way chickens typically view
aprons. When HENHOUSE reporters followed up with Carol
Rawle, who handled her friend with such care, she gave us
this incredible update:

"By the way, Alice molted and grew all her feathers back
and has never lost them again, and she has since moved up
to near the top in the pecking order. I now have a Brahma
with the feather problems and she refuses to wear an apron,
spending days on end removing it (or until I remove it) out of
contact frustration."

"Sorry about taking so long to respond but I thought you
were a spammer."

"c"

DON'T

JUST DON'T.

HENHOUSE

DON'T FEATHER EXTENSIONS

Feather hair extensions are sold as fashion ornaments, but these ornamental feathers don't just fall from the sky off any ol' bird. Feather extensions for hair come from roosters raised for this sole purpose, and in pretty cruddy conditions as you may have gathered by now.

The largest American supplier of feather extensions is Whiting Farms (Colorado). Karen Davis of United Poultry Concerns wrote of Whiting Farms, "According to the company, 'Each rooster has only a small number of tail feathers that can be used for sales — sometimes none, sometimes five or six.' Up to 1,500 roosters may be killed by Whiting Farms each week for the fashion industry. The dead roosters are then trashed, like garbage. 'They aren't good for anything else,' [said] company president Thomas Whiting…'"

If you or Aerosmith (don't wanna miss a thing, here) are wearing feather hair extensions, give it a rest, in peace.

DO

THE HEN WHO LAYS THE GOLDEN L'EGGS!

Seasholtz

THE SKETCHES OF SHAPPY SEASHOLTZ

DON'T
OGGLE THE JOGGERS

PHOTO BY JAMES DOBSON (PEAKDISTRICTONLINE.CO.UK)

DO
KEEP JOGGING

HOME GIRLS

KINGSTON, WA

(ALL PHOTOS IN HOME GIRLS BY MALCOLM SMITH
(MALCOLMSMITHPHOTO.COM)

LADIES & GENTLEMEN,
THE WOMEN WHO INSPIRED HENHOUSE...

AC/DC

THIS IS 12-YEAR-OLD AC IN THE FRONT, and her sister, DC (back right). After their rooster, Garth Gentleman, was killed in the line of duty by a slick coyote, it was AC who stepped up to the plate to look after the rest of the girls. She was a rather plump and respected leader, never giving in to the temptation of using a motorized scooter to shuttle her from spot to spot. AC passed away peacefully before HENHOUSE went to press, but she is fully aware we are bound to be successful thanks to her guidance and coaching. Just look at that pose, ladies. Gorgeous to the end.

THOUGH AC/DCs DAYS AS FAMOUS MUSICIANS have come to an end (roost in peace, AC), DC (pictured here) is still holding it down for the full-feathered rockers, often found belting out lyrical jams from their platinum debut, "Black and Fat." Recently, surviving member, DC, was heard in the dust bath proudly delivering their chart-topping title track, "Black and fat! / I need a snack! / I'm in the garden 'cause I like to scratch! / I'm all cluck! / No quack! / My favorite corn in the world is cracked!" So special.

A candid look at DC sunbathing in the yard with her friend, Radish.

Here's a closer look at Rhode Island Radish, the five-year-old foodaphile.

RHODE ISLAND RADISH
&
THE JUDDS

IT'S EXTREMELY DIFFICULT to tell Rhode Island Radish the foodaphile apart from her sister, The Judds. They are almost identical in every way, except that The Judds (which is actually just one individual Rhode Island Red) believes "Love Can Build A Bridge..." to the DMV. That's right, if The Judds could get her driver's license, she would. She loves greeting the car and watching the car leave, and standing in the way of the car, and making forget-me-not piles on top of the car. It is actually her dream to, one day, drive the car.

THIS IS RADISH WAITING for the giant octopus (it's a work truck from our landscaping company in Kingston, WA, Sea Stone Yard Works). You're sure to find Radish pacing right here every early evening in anticipation of all those lawn clippings. Here we see Radish waiting for the octopus to get home with the goods (she thinks it's an octopus because it's so much bigger than the car. Yes, I am aware that that doesn't make sense; try telling it to Radish).

Fast Priscilla at her most elegant.

THIS IS FAST PRISCILLA. See that look in her eye? She wasn't born with it, the coyotes caused it. Fast Priscilla has witnessed the deaths of many babies and friends by way of coyote. She seems to be forever on guard or airborne. Impersonal to humans, sharp, stealth, organized and a fantastic mother, Fast Priscilla does enjoy the company of the other girls when she's not busy brooding, but when it's baby-makin' time, everybody back off! Today, she is in the barn inventing booby traps for predators. I have asked her to be humane about it. She locked the door.

HERE'S A TOUCHING SHOT OF DC on a walk with young Epic (the sole survivor of a clutch of 12 chicks). It took the girls in the henhouse a long time to accept this self-reliant beauty, but when the new rooster,

THIS IS OLIVE JUICE. She begged us to list her as DJ Static because of her feather arrangement and penchant for daytime raves, but we wanted you to meet her sans the many phases she is growing through faster than we can shake a glow stick at. Olive is a natural born, sly and fearless leader. She is fun, self-advised and marches to the beat of whatever record suits her taste on any given day (typically Lemon Jelly and Caribou).

What with DC being the oldest, she can get a bit bossy. Olive Juice is usually fairly understanding, but sometimes it's like, "Ya know what, DC, talk to the fluff."

HOW KIND IS IT OF OLIVE JUICE to share a blurry edge of the spotlight with our two growing geese and four ducks (The Colonel & Mrs. Marple, Butters, Puddin, Smuckers, and The Legend of Greystoke — who recently came out to us as being grey, which we're accepting).

Emails to adopt more hens just went out to some of the websites listed in "Hen's Health," and we're lookin' forward to the new additions at HENHOUSE Headquarters. As for everyone already here at HENHOUSE, we sure thank you for having so much fun with us, and here's to a wholesome practice.

When we stop just knowing how to live in an all-around healthy manner and actually put that knowledge into practice, well, the consequences are immediate.

...And the roost is history

THE THANK YA-DOODLE-DOOs! [FORGIVE ME THAT]

Consider this moment, this text right here, sincere and boundless thanks for each of HENHOUSE's many contributors. Visit their websites, blogs, forums, galleries and social networking pages. Look them up. Start a sanctuary. Adopt a wholesome practice. All photos, comics and text were printed with permission from the artists.

Most of the credits occur in-the-moment throughout HENHOUSE, but additional recognition is due for some folks who offered untold hours of work, directly or indirectly, from which HENHOUSE benefitted in some way. So, thank you quite much:

Captain Derrick Brown of Write Bloody Publishing. Photo wingman, Daniel Lisi. The artist currently known as Brandon Lyon; his design and layout caused this creation to come full circle. Adam Weightman. Nik Ewing. Patient Bill Jonas. Cover designer Anthony Wyborny. Mary and Bert of ChickenRunRescue.org and their comrade, Karen Davis, of United Poultry Concerns (none of whom care to be associated with this publication, but for whose outside efforts I am unable to let go thankless). Jeffrey McDaniel, whose quote comes from his book The Forgiveness Parade© Manic D Press, 1998. Jenny Woods and People for the Ethical Treatment of Animals. Sybil Fix. "Pat" from backyardchickens.com. Oakland, CA citizen, Tim Anderson. Generous comic artist, Adrian Raeside. Alexzander Benavidez. Novella Carpenter. The kindness, fact-checking and proofreading skills of chicken-showing journalist Danielle Pope, Ronnie K. Stephens, and Sir Douglas Swaim of the Serene Rehab Clinic for English Lit. majors. Cooptain Berg Danielson. The Incredible Hollie Chastain, Kieth Pitts, and Jennifer Davis for the extra attention and fantastic artwork. Our fast and brilliant friend, Tim Sanders. Anyone who took the time to offer submissions and input. Also, Vipassana meditators (dhamma.org). And, Extra Special V.I.P. Platinum Elite First Class A-List Photography thanks are in order for Jaclyn Jularbal, Ashley Knight, Denise Dawson, Kara Mannix and James Dobson.

Finally, and once more, thank you Danielle Pope for bringing all the loose ends together when it counted most. A better blessing than you, for HENHOUSE, seems unlikely.

Stay coo.

Your fine feathered editors,
BUDDY WAKEFIELD & STEPHEN SNOOK

97

WORKS

CITED

1: BRITTON CLOUSE, MARY. "Increased Demand for Placement of 'Urban Farm' Animals." Chicken Run Rescue. (2012.) Retrieved 19 July 2012. <http://www.brittonclouse.com/chickenrunrescue/surrender_chart.pdf>.

2-4: BRITTON CLOUSE, MARY. "Reasons Not to Purchase Chicks from Hatcheries." Chicken Run Rescue. (n.d.) Retrieved 19 July 2012. <http://chickenrunrescue.org/#hatcheries>.

5: KOKOLAKIS, SMITH, EVANS. "Aerial Alarm Calling By Male Fowl (Gallus gallus) Reveals Subtle New Mechanisms of Risk Management." 22 April 2010. Macquarie University. Retrieved 19 July 2012. <http://dx.doi.org/10.1016/j.anbehav.2010.03.013>.

6: MACON, STEVEN C. "Chickens." Grass In The Backyard. 6 September 2011. Retrieved 19 July 2012. <http://grassinthebackyard.blogspot.ca/2011/09/chickens.html>.

7: Quotation. CYPHER, JEAN. "Stray chicken came first, then the eggs, for accidental urban farmer Patricia Arnao." NY Daily News. 15 August 2009. Retrieved 19 July 2012. <http://articles.nydailynews.com/2009-08-15/entertainment/17933936_1_chicks-shipping-hatcheries>.

8-10: BRITTON CLOUSE, MARY. "Reasons Not to Purchase Chicks from Hatcheries." Chicken Run Rescue. (n.d.) Retrieved 19 July 2012. <http://chickenrunrescue.org/#hatcheries>.

11: CANADIAN POULTRY CONSULTANTS Ltd. "Diagnosis of Poultry Disease." 2005. Retrieved 19 July 2012. <http://www.canadianpoultry.ca/index.htm>.

12: HAYES, RICH. "Antibiotics Overused in Chickens." The Baltimore Sun. 23 July 2001. Retrieved 19 July 2012. <http://articles.baltimoresun.com/2001-07-23/news/0107230006_1_antibiotics-chicken-house-chicken-factories>.

13-15: ROBBINS, JOHN. The Food Revolution. Conari Press: Boston, 2001. 195-196. Print.

16: SAVORY, HOCKING, MANN, and MAXWELL. "Is Broiler Breeder Welfare Improved by Using Qualitative Rather Than Qualitative Food Restriction to Limit Growth Rate?" Animal Welfare. 1996. 106. Print.

17: KNOWLES, T.G. and WILKINS, L.G. "The Problem of Broken Bones During Handling of Laying Hens: A Review." Poultry Science. 1998. Print.

BREED LIST
(For those eyeballing their favorite chicks)

Cover: *Blue Frizzle bantam hen* **1-2:** *Golden-laced Wyandotte hen* **3:** *Silver Sebright bantam cock* **6:** *(top) Silver-laced Wyandotte hens, (bottom) Rhode Island Red hen with two Rhode Island White hens* **7:** *(top) Three White Plymouth Rock hens, (bottom) White Polish cock* **8:** *New Hampshire cock* **9:** *(top) Non-standard Rhode Island Red hen, (bottom) Rhode Island Red hen, with friends* **10:** *Mottled Japanese bantam cock, with friends* **11:** *Rosecomb crossbreed cock, with hen* **12:** *Blue Silkie bantam hen with Silver Duckwing Old English Game bantam cock* **13:** *Silver Duckwing Old English Game bantam cock and hen* **14:** *Blue Silkie bantam hen* **15:** *Black Australorp cock* **16:** *Silver Duckwing Old English Game bantam cock* **17:** *Black Silkie bantam hen* **18:** *Silver Duckwing Old English Game bantam hen* **20:** *Buff Orpington hen* **23:** *New Hampshire hen* **24:** *Blue Frizzle bantam hen* **25:** *(top left) Bearded Buff-Laced Polish bantam hen, (top right) White Frizzle cock, (middle left) Wheaten Old English Game bantam hen and her mixed brood, (bottom left) Golden-laced Brahma bantam hen, (bottom right) Partridge Chantecler cock* **26:** *(top left) Dark Brahma hen, (top right) White Crested Black Non-Bearded Polish cock, (bottom) White Crested Black Non-Bearded Polish hen* **27:** *(left) White Leghorn hen, (top right) White Crested Black Non-Bearded Polish cock, (bottom right) Silver Laced Non-Bearded Polish hen* **28:** *Non-standard Rhode Island Red* **29:** *Painted Leghorn cock* **30:** *Jersey Giant Hen* **31:** *Delaware hen with chick* **32:** *Delaware cock* **33:** *Rhode Island Red cock* **34:** *Blue Ameraucana hen* **35:** *White Indian Game cock and hens* **36:** *Barred Plymouth Rock hen* **41:** *Buff Orpington hen* **43:** *Black Old English Game hen and chicks* **45:** *(left) Rhode Island White hen and chicks, (right) Rhode Island Red hen* **46:** *Barred Plymouth Rock Chick, Buff Orpington bantam pullet and Barred Plymouth Rock bantam pullet* **52-53:** *Rhode Island Red hen* **54:** *Buff Orpington hen* **55:** *(top) Buff Orpington hen with Golden-laced Wyandotte hen, (middle) Buff Orpington hen with Barred Plymouth Rock hen and Golden-laced Wyandotte hen, (bottom) Buff Orpington hen with Golden-laced Wyandotte hen* **56-57:** *Silver Sebright bantam cock* **66-67:** *Rhode Island Red hens* **68:** *New Hampshire cock* **71:** *Flock of non-standard Rhode Island Red and White hens* **72-73:** *Delaware cock* **74:** *Dead and live commercial Cornish Cross broiler birds* **75:** *Debeaked commercial Leghorn laying hens* **77:** *Commercial Cornish Cross broiler chickens* **86:** *Golden-laced Wyandotte hen* **87:** *(top) Rhode Island Red cock, (bottom) Golden and Silver-laced Wyandotte hens* **89:** *White Plymouth Rock hen* **90:** *Barred Plymouth Rock hen* **91:** *Black Australorp hens, with Rhode Island Red hen* **92:** *Rhode Island Red hen* **93:** *Mottled Sebright bantam hen, (bottom right) Black Australorp hen with Black Old English Game bantam hen* **94-95:** *Barred Plymouth Rock hen* **96:** *Black Australorp hen with Rhode Island Red hen and Barred Plymouth Rock hen*